THORNTON WILDER

LITERATURE AND LIFE: AMERICAN WRITERS

Selected list of titles:

Complete list of titles in the series available from publisher on request. Some titles are also in paperback.

THORNTON WILDER

David Castronovo

UNGAR • NEW YORK

1986
The Ungar Publishing Company
370 Lexington Avenue, New York, N.Y. 10017

Printed in the United States of America

Library of Congress Cataloging-in-Publication Data

Castronovo, David.
  Thornton Wilder.

  (Literature and life. American writers)
  Bibliography: p.
  Includes index.
  1. Wilder, Thornton, 1897–1975—Criticism and
interpretation. I. Title. II. Series.
PS3545.I345Z58   1986   818'.5209   86-19255
ISBN 0-8044-2119-6

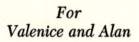

For
Valenice and Alan

Contents

Chronology

1897	Thornton Niven Wilder is born in Madison, Wisconsin, on April 17.
1906	For six months Thornton attends school in Hong Kong where his father is Consul General.
1906–9	Is enrolled in school at Berkeley, California; enjoys first taste of drama at the Greek Theatre.
1910	Returns to China and attends the China Inland Mission Boys and Girls School at Chefoo; studies classics.
1912	At Thacher School in California; acts in school plays.
1913–15	Transfers to Berkeley High School; reads widely in modern literature. Begins writing three-minute plays.
1915	Is sent by father, Amos, to Oberlin College in Ohio. Continues writing and earns indifferent grades.
1917–20	Completes undergraduate study at Yale; active in campus literary societies; wins Bradford Brinton Award for *The Trumpet Shall Sound*, a play derived from Jonson's *The Alchemist*.
1918–19	Serves in U.S. Coast Artillary Corps.
1920	Studies archaeology in Rome at the American

Academy; finishes European stay with language study in Paris.

1922   Teaches at the Lawrenceville School in New Jersey. At work on *Memoirs of a Roman Student*, later to be published as *The Cabala*.

1925–26   At Princeton University for a master's degree in French literature.

1927   Back at Lawrenceville as master of Davis House; *The Bridge of San Luis Rey* is published and enthusiastically reviewed; becomes best seller.

1928   Pulitzer Prize for *The Bridge*; remains at Lawrenceville and tours Europe in summer with three of his students.

1929   Lecture tour across country; begins construction of the "House the Bridge Built" in Hamden, Connecticut.

1930   Begins to teach writing and classics in translation at the University of Chicago. Publishes *The Woman of Andros*.

1931   *The Long Christmas Dinner and Other Plays* published.

1934   Meets Gertrude Stein in Chicago.

1935   *Heaven's My Destination* published.

1936   Amos Wilder dies; Wilder leaves Chicago "to be a WRITER!" Spends time with Stein and Toklas at Bilignin; visits Freud in Vienna.

1938   *Our Town* produced on Broadway. Pulitzer Prize for drama.

1942   *The Skin of Our Teeth* performed in New York; author enlists in Army Air Intelligence.

1943   Pulitzer Prize for *Skin*.

1946   Mother dies.

1947   Litt.D. from Yale.

1948   Publishes *The Ides of March*.

1949   At the Aspen Goethe Festival in Colorado

where he delivers "World Literature and the Modern Mind."

1950–51 Charles Eliot Norton Professor at Harvard. LL.D. from Harvard in 1951.

1952 Gold Medal from the National Institute of Arts and Letters.

1955 *The Matchmaker*—revised version of *The Merchant of Yonkers*—on Broadway. *The Alcestiad* runs at the Edinburgh Festival.

1957 Receives German Booksellers' Peace Prize and criticizes literary elitism in his acceptance speech.

1962 *Plays for Bleecker Street*—including *Someone from Assisi, Infancy*, and *Childhood*—performed in New York.

1963 Working on a novel called *Anthracite*, later to be titled *The Eighth Day*. Freedom Medal.

1964 *Hello, Dolly!*, with music and lyrics by Jerry Herman, runs on Broadway. Wilder has no part in the adaptation.

1965 Receives National Book Committee's Medal for Literature at the White House.

1967 *The Eighth Day* is published.

1973 *Theophilus North* is published.

1975 Dies in the "House the Bridge Built" in Hamden, Connecticut, on December 7.

1985 *The Journals of Thornton Wilder 1939–1961* published.

1

The Skin of His Teeth: Wilder's Career and Reputation

Thornton Wilder is a protean writer whose literary contemporaries in America are more easily appreciated,
clearly identifiable, and artistically stable. An adapter of
styles and assumer of disguises, Wilder is unlike writers
whose imprints are recognizable over their lifetimes and
connected with certain localities and social climates.
Moving restlessly from setting to setting and style to
style in his novels and plays, he is not the kind of artist
who stakes a claim to a territory or a group. Wilder's
peers often reveal their identities through their characteristic atmospheres, dominions that they rule over for
decades. Hemingway's fictional reports on Michigan and
expatriate Europe establish him as a writer and remain
in the minds of his readers as permanent features of his
art. With many other American writers, the story is
about the same—the artist is attached to his landscapes:
Fitzgerald's Midwest, New York, and Riviera; Faulkner's Yoknapatawpha County; Lewis's Middle America;
O'Hara's New York and Gibbsville; Cheever's Shady
Hill; Bellow's Chicago; Updike's Pennsylvania. Wilder is
out of step with this devotion to reporting on claimed
places, studying certain types of people, and accumula-
ting pieces of reality that constitute a vision of a time and
place.

A fabricator rather than an observer of the American or European scene, a student and a taster of cultures rather than a working expatriate on the Continent, Wilder is something of an oddity in American letters. He is all but alone in his hothouse craftsmanship, his conjured settings, and his bookish approach to creating characters and backgrounds. Wilder Country is best described by offering an ill-assorted list of places that are either synthetic recreations of past civilizations or highly stylized representations of America and Europe: ancient and modern Rome, eighteenth-century Peru, Atlantic City, Illinois, New Hampshire, ancient Greece, Yonkers, Newport, and Kansas City. No pattern can be found in this list, least of all the now classic motifs of Hemingway pursuing adventure or Fitzgerald following the rich or Faulkner tracing his moral origins.

Nicola Chiaramonte, an incisive commentator on Wilder's art, offered a backhanded compliment in 1955 when he wrote that Wilder was "disgusted by the fact that the world is real rather than imaginary." He went on to say that Wilder "is not one of the great, nor does he presume to be. He is a moralistic *pasticheur* [and] his morality is exclusively related to the imaginary world that he likes to create by realistic means." He pronounced Wilder to be "the only contemporary writer who is literate in the European sense . . . the humanistic sense."[1] Such a mixture of praise and qualification is a good starting point for evaluating Wilder's literary identity.

As a student of archaeology in Rome in the 1920s, the young Wilder started a relationship with the European past that separated him from the nativists and modernist reporters among his contemporaries; he became a digger and researcher, a voyager in imaginary settings, at a time when the best talents were involved with the immediate situation of the modern protagonist. Wilder looked down the corridors of time while others examined the texture of their age. The twentieth century was not large enough to contain his themes—and American experience was a subject he came to after a few books. He wrote explicitly about philosophical and moral questions at a time when restraint, understatement, and indirection were the approaches of his best contemporaries. And unlike the major writers of his era, he was generally unconcerned with originality as an end in itself: he had no reservations about adapting, absorbing, and accepting the European tradition—so long as it suited his purposes. His writing life was an example of the idea of slow development of styles and themes, comradeship with masters, and imitation. The anxieties of European influences were with him throughout his career, enriching his work and life, haunting him, sometimes distracting him, and frequently casting shadows on his reputation. In writing about Joyce and Mann in his *Journals*, he summed up his experience by describing that of others: "Book-writing-men—feeding on writing men. And, of course, in all this I am thinking of myself."

The author of *Our Town*—a play that has unfortunately entered our consciousness as if it were a protracted dramatization of the Pledge of Allegiance—had a mind that was distinctly un-American in its approach to the writer's craft and vocation. That mind endured in the midst of the threats of American literary and social life. Wilder's career was pursued against the resisting currents of twentieth-century American sensibility and taste; his books are a series of affronts to the modern way of being an American artist. Not driven to escape provincial settings and become an expatriate, not contemptuous of bourgeois values and past pieties, not inflamed with hatred of American power and wealth, not an ethnic or a regionalist, not daring in his treatment of politics or sex, not a man of action, not a self-celebrator, Wilder seems to deliver something that his readers are unprepared for.

Wilder's early life and its conflicts foreshadow the complex and problematic nature of his work: cheerful submission to authority and the yearning for adventure and exoticism, Americanism and the attraction of European culture, Protestant rectitude and aestheticism —these are the themes that take the field both in childhood and later life. Amos Wilder, the author's father, had been reared in Maine and bred up to the Calvinist mission of dedication to public causes, devotion to family life, and avoidance of frivolity. A sententious man of his time, Amos embodied the faults of the up-and-doing professional: distrust of the arts, rigidity, censoriousness, and love of high-flown pronouncements about man's inner life. A Yale graduate and Ph.D. in political science, he began a career as a teacher before switching to journalism. Marriage and family life started at the time he bought an interest in a Madison, Wisconsin, newspaper. Amos became the scourge of corrupt politicians and the liquor interests. As husband and father he began a fairly typical reign as a benign bully—indoctrinating, intimidating, and condemning—but doing so in a genial tone of voice. The newspaper income soon proved inadequate to meet the needs of a growing family, but a good connection brought Amos a post as consul general in Hong Kong.

Of the Wilder children—Thornton, Amos, Janet, Charlotte, and Isabel—Thornton Niven, born in Wisconsin in 1897, was the greatest source of anxiety for "Papa." The record of Wilder's childhood was filled with gentle paternal admonitions: Thornton's "artistic temperament," his dreamy irresponsibility, his oddity of manner and self-absorption alarmed Amos. Papa pronounced Thornton's early literary efforts to be "carving on olive pits."[2] He hoped that Thornton would not "lay too much stress on Greek or any other plays. I must hold that the man who does a thing is more important than the fellow who shows how it is done."[3] Sometimes he was even pleased with the young boy: "I rejoice that Thornton is able to water an occasional lawn."[4]

Thornton was also subjected to shifts from school to school. After starting his education in Madison, he was brought to Hong Kong in 1906 and enrolled in a German school. Wilder's mother, an imaginative woman of taste and culture who had been frustrated as a young girl in her aspirations to study medicine, disliked everything about the China arrangements; the constant social obligations and her fears about educational prospects for the children soon drove her back to the States—this time to Berkeley, California. Thornton now took part in little-theater productions and studied music. But by 1909 Papa summoned the family, except for brother Amos, back to China. Thornton and his sister Charlotte were sent to the China Inland Mission Boys and Girls School in Chefoo, an institution that emphasized classics and muscular Christianity—including compulsory cricket (a game from which Wilder got himself exempt).[5] Here he met Henry Luce, the future *Time* mogul. He developed a rather lively personality and a reputation for being eccentric.

When Thornton was sixteen, another change came. He left China to attend the Thacher School, a fancy prep school where he continued to polish his reputation as an oddity, an arty type, and drama enthusiast. (Papa, Gilbert Harrison reports, would not permit Thornton to play the part of Lady Bracknell in *The Importance of Being Earnest*).[6] In 1913 still another adjustment was made—Berkeley High School and home life with his mother and sisters. The home—minus Papa—was now dominated by Mrs. Wilder and her love of European culture and art. Thornton discovered modern writers like Proust and Mann, became an avid theatergoer, and shared his ardors with a mother whom he referred to as "Our Lady of Florence." He also conceived of a series of three-minute plays that he worked on during his college years. His conceptions were exotic and atypical of most teenage literary enterprises: instead of writing about personal experience, he chose to create a strange, non-referential world of fantasies. One of these plays takes place inside a Renaissance painting; another is set in Saint Francis's Italy.

Such material suggests the kind of writer Wilder was to become; it also points to his boyhood conflict. The child with Protestant morality in his heart had a mother who was signalling him to earthly beauty. The small-town American boy was snatched from California to China. The upper-class ambience of Thacher was replaced by the local high school. Boyhood plans were vetoed or modified by Papa. Nothing, it seems, could be counted on for long. Wilder submitted himself to whatever authority seemed most forceful at the time. No rebel or fractious adolescent, he managed to be malleable and creative. But his willingness to adjust makes us wonder where his identity was located. Was he moralistic like his father or aesthetic like his mother? When it came to locales, what did he identify as his own? Did he find his being while running near the seacoast in Shantung where "a row of sycamores and gingko trees enclosed a semicircle of noble tombs called the Grove of Ancestors"?[7] Or was he Papa's American boy watering a lawn? The shifting and conflicting signals of boyhood produced a writer who could not rest content with one kind of atmosphere, style, or set of opinions.

When Wilder finished high school, Amos presented the next surprise—not Yale, but Oberlin College. The grander institution was considered to be too worldly and sophisticated for the poorly disciplined and vaguely focused boy. Oberlin—a Congregationalist plain-living-and-high-thinking college—was more to Papa's taste; it satisfied Thornton too. The peculiar richness of Oberlin —with its compulsory Chapel, fine humanistic curriculum, and social progressivism—was very accessible to a boy whose father was a Puritan do-gooder and whose mother was a culture seeker. Wilder took courses with English Professor Charles H. A. Wager, a distinguished teacher whose staunch Protestantism was combined with a generous understanding of Catholic and pagan civilization. Wilder wrote a poem in the Oberlin magazine about this mentor. Stilted in its phrasing, it is nevertheless touching in its anxiety. The young versifier has borne away "The Spark" of his teacher—"Enriched and freed from fear, thy face toward mine—as Vergil led the hooded Florentine." Richard Goldstone comments that Wager-Vergil was "respectably garbed in New England Puritan attire"[8]—which is to say that Wilder had found an authority who syncretized New England and Europe, Papa and "Our Lady of Florence." He is freed from fear when he finds some person who makes art moral and morality attractive.

At Oberlin, Wilder continued to cut a figure and cultivate the manner of the aesthete; one fellow student, Frederick Artz, found him to be an exotic anachronism on campus, a witty epigrammist whose style was like that of an Enlightenment abbé.[9] With Papa at a distance, the young man also socialized a great deal and spent more time on his writing than on course work. The results showed in a mediocre academic record. At the end of his second year, another shift came: Amos decided to send "hopeless Thornton"[10] to Yale. When he started at New Haven, without Junior status because of the weak grades, the academic situation was the same: writing at the expense of studying. While juggling a demanding program as an English major, he pursued such extracurricular gratifications as the Elizabethan Club and the *Lit*—the first a social paradise for a writer in search of talk, the second a place to publish his one-act plays. Papa, meanwhile, had Thornton paying his dues to the workaday world: the student went several nights a week to study business subjects at a local institute. On

top of that, Thornton started writing and reviewing for a
New York paper; this led to running to the city and wandering around Greenwich Village. And then one of the
besetting problems of his life appeared—his love of ex-
citing company. The transfer student from the Midwest
came under the influence of the more glamorous Yale
types. The writer who dissipated so much time in the
1930s and 1940s with New York literary people began
his social career among the well-born and cultivated un-
dergraduates. He was impressed by the "golden casual-
ness" of young men who traveled with Stephen Vincent
Benét, bought deluxe-edition books, and seemed to belong at Oxford. Wilder, "obsequious and Uriah Heepish"
in the presence of people who were not middle class and
who were in a position to judge his work, was aware of
his ambiguous position. "It takes one from the jaded
middle class, one too used to pinching and window shop-
ping and chatting with grocers' sons, to really appraise
the amenities, and timbres of such a group."[11] The
alien's perspective—here a matter of admiration-
condescension—is another example of Wilder's unsta-
ble situation.

At Yale, he won the Bradford Brinton Award for
The Trumpet Shall Sound, a play suggested by Ben
Jonson's *The Alchemist.* This allegory of possession and
justice, about what happens when servants take over
their master's house, is interesting for its moralistic emphasis and its frank use of another playwright's material.
During the Yale years he also worked on the three-
minute plays. Some of these efforts are rather heavily
and indigestibly flavored with biblical, medieval, and fin
de siècle styles.

Clearly, a practical man like Amos did not know
what to do with a son involved in such experiments.
World War I had briefly interrupted Thornton's Yale career and caused him to spend some time in the Coast

Guard at Newport. But what would the "dear boy" do
with his life? Fortunately for Thornton, his mother came
up with the idea of a year of study at the American Academy in Rome. Amos provided nine hundred dollars for
the year, and Thornton then set off on a budget version
of the American gentleman's postgraduate tour of the
Old World. In Rome he acquired a light coating of Latin
and archaeology and gained entrance to a few salons.
Gilbert Harrison reports that there was a powerful romantic experience with a woman—and a painful rejection that is later registered in his first novel, *The Cabala*.[12] During his year abroad, Wilder did not acquire
the tastes and attitudes of the expatriates. After a while,
he even longed for home and his father's authority:
"Your queer 'aesthetic,' over-cerebral son may yet turn
out to be your most fundamental New Englander."
Papa, of course, wanted the trip to pay: he searched up a
job as a French teacher at the Blairstown School and
sent Thornton to Paris to prepare by studying the language. Living on ninety cents a day, Thornton got a
mere taste of literary France, including visits to cafés,
calls on his Yale friends, and a stop at Sylvia Beach's
Shakespeare and Company.

When he returned to the States, the teaching appointment turned out to be at Lawrenceville School. As
a job, it was a considerable source of satisfaction; he became a popular, dedicated teacher and housemaster.
The man of European tastes enjoyed helping his students by tutoring, advising, and even doing day-to-day
tasks like chauffeuring and monitoring. While other
members of his generation were escaping Anglo-Saxon
America, Wilder seemed to be moving on a different
path: "There is no longer any sense of incompleteness or
strangeness about any pleasure I get out of America."[13]
And yet the creative activity of the period, especially
The Cabala and *The Bridge of San Luis Rey*, suggests a

strange mental distance from the concerns of his New
Jersey colleagues and students. While working as a
prep-school master, he was voyaging in Rome and Peru.

Thornton started the 1920s in Europe, moved to
New Jersey, and ended in Europe: during the middle
stretch of time, he became a celebrity. *The Bridge of
San Luis Rey* brought immediate fame and money, but it
did not represent any radical departure from Wilder's
earlier efforts or any attempt to write popular fiction.
This highly wrought, exquisite book was a predictable
second novel for the writer who had published a very literary first novel. The first work, originally to be called
Memoirs of a Roman Student and later changed to *The
Cabala,* is about a group of self-absorbed patricians, each
enmeshed in a special kind of frustration. Begun at Lawrenceville, the novel was finished during a two-year
leave of absence from the school, a period during which
Wilder had decided to take an M.A. in romance lan-
guages at Princeton. The book has the aroma of scholar-
ship combined with the delicate craftsmanship of a series
of miniature portraits. Denying the influences of his Roman sojourn, Wilder insisted that his work owed more to
"Proust, La Bruyère, the memoirs of the Duke of Saint-
Simon, Thomas Mann, and Lytton Strachey."[14] (Such
influences account for Hemingway's respectfully delivered remark that Wilder's inspiration came from "the
library.")

The Bridge, coming promptly in 1927, is similarly
fabricated: Wilder of course had never seen Peru and
had spent most of his time during the period with New
Yorkers, his family, and his Lawrenceville charges. He
conjured up three portraits of unsuccessful lovers and
then framed them with an ironic discussion of why these
pathetic romantics died on the same day (in the first
draft, the date was Wilder's birthday) in a catastrophic
accident. Part of the reason for Wilder's success can be
found in his very modern treatment of love and death:

like Hemingway and Fitzgerald, despite the differences in style and atmosphere, Wilder treated people who are ravaged by the pain of desire and by the knowledge that human affections move along short circuits. No fuzzy sentimentalist or optimistic distorter of human fate in *The Bridge*, Wilder took his place—albeit a strange one—beside his contemporaries. Edmund Wilson felt the influence of Proust, yet acknowledged that Wilder had a manner all his own. There is "an edge that is peculiar to himself, an edge that is never incompatible with the attainment of a consummate felicity."[15] For Wilson, Wilder's Peru is "solid, incandescent, distinct." But the praise from America's foremost essayist was not unmixed with prescient warnings about Wilder's shortcomings and likely problems with American audiences. Wilson remarked that some of Wilder's passages were "pure Proust," and therefore among his least successful. He continued that Wilder "took" a "formula for emotion" from Proust rather than a style: the very word formula seems loaded and very deftly gave notice to a young writer about the dangers ahead. Was Wilder heading for a career of repetition? Wilson mentioned that *The Cabala* perhaps had one hopeless love too many in its pages. And then, finally, there were the settings of the books: wasn't it time to bring prose and sensibility to bear on the American scene? "I wish," Wilson wrote, "that he would study the diverse elements that go to make the United States and give us *their* national portraits. Mr. Wilder already knows Europe, and he also knows something of the Orient; and now we need him at home. I believe that this player on plaintive stops has more than one tune in his flute."[16] An amalgam of shrewd advice and obtuseness in regard to Wilder's great gift for exoticism and fabrication, this comment is a prediction of Wilder's discomfort in America. (In a letter to Wilson dated August 24, 1928, Wilder referred to the criticism as "good rich food.")

Wilson's kindly and sincere urgings in 1928 may very well have caused Wilder to turn to America in two of his greatest one-act plays, *The Happy Journey to Trenton and Camden* and *Pullman Car Hiawatha*. These works are the first of many important returns to the States, but like later ones—*Our Town, The Eighth Day*—they are far different from the work of the local colorist or the social chronicler. Both plays effectively present time passing and people's epiphanies as they are sped through stylized landscapes. Using his eye to create settings that are so typical that they are terrifying, he accelerates his people—on a train and in a car— through the ordinary joys and agonies of all places and times. Evidently Wilder did not find it easy to see universal patterns in the confines of his own country. "Already," he remarked in an interview, "in the one-act plays, I had become aware of how difficult it is to invest one's contemporary world with the same kind of imaginative life one has extended to those removed in time and place."[17] His next book was the *Woman of Andros* (1930), a novel set in the first century A.D. The work was a flash point in his career, a quiet and suavely written narrative that set off a reaction out of proportion to its worth or its shortcomings.

After *The Bridge* Wilder enjoyed success, but in his own unassuming way. Never one to let fame go to his head, he continued for a time at Lawrenceville, teaching French, helping boys to get train tickets home for the holidays, and enjoying his campus distinction as a bestselling author. Harrison notes that "New York publishers practically camp in tents on Lawrenceville lawns, pushing for Thornton's signature on a contract."[18] Socially, Wilder was beginning to move among the golden people of the twenties. He was invited by Fitzgerald and Zelda to a house near Wilmington, Delaware, here to talk and drink with Edmund Wilson. The critic found him "extremely responsive," but "sharply and firmly non-soluble."[19] He developed a friendship with Gene Tunney, the heavyweight-champion boxer who liked literature. Together, they took a hiking trip through France and Germany in 1928—and provided joking material much later for Gore Vidal.[20] Vidal teased Wilder about being a homosexual—and voiced a conviction that many critics, commentators, and friends shared. But throughout his life Wilder himself recoiled from displaying his sexuality in any form, preferring to evade categories just as he evaded easy critical descriptions or typing. Wilder's geniality and frankness about likes and dislikes were strangely combined with a withdrawal from self-publicizing and autobiographical soul bearing. He was a man of his age in that he preferred disguises and personae to romantic self-celebration and examination.

During his adult life, Wilder retained the sense of responsibility to family and society that Papa had so well inculcated. After the *Bridge*, he repaid a loan to his father, put his mother on an allowance, and started building a family house outside New Haven. In 1929 he honored a lecture tour contract to promote *The Bridge*, a hideously demanding schedule of one hundred forty-four appearances across the country. No sooner was it complete than he signed on at the University of Chicago to teach classics in translation and advanced composition. The offer of a position had come from an old Oberlin friend, Robert Hutchins, the new president of the university who would bring Chicago's reputation into the first rank during the 1930s. Wilder settled in with his usual good humor and dedication to a task. He worked diligently on his courses, developed a notable rapport with students, and made the young people his companions. Although not familiar in his dealings with students, he was nevertheless willing to spend evenings in restaurants and apartments, talking about literature and their concerns. He also moved with a moneyed older set, people in the arts who lived on the North Side. He wrote a good part of *The Woman of Andros* while living in these congenial settings.

But eight months after the book was published in 1930, the first major crisis of his career came in the form of a review in the liberal *New Republic*. Mike Gold, an editor of the left-wing *New Masses*, had been asked by acting editor Malcolm Cowley to write a guest review. Although Edmund Wilson had offered his characteristic reasoned guidance, Gold greeted Wilder's third novel —and by extension his first two—with a meat axe. In the heated-up prose of the Communist ideologue, Gold accused Wilder's work of being effete and irresponsible. Like some Spiro Agnew of the Left, Gold put together an attack that combined open invective and innuendo: "Wilder: Prophet of the Genteel Christ"[21] refers to the novelist as "The Emily Post of Culture"; the Greek characters in *The Woman of Andros* are called "homosexual figures in graceful gowns moving archaically among the lilies." Wilder, "the poet of a small sophisticated class," is accused of being empty of ideas and social content; his religious themes are reduced to being the teachings of "Jesus Christ, The First British Gentleman." The sufferings that are drawn so tautly across Wilder's plot are "little lavender tragedies." When faced with Wilder's mastery of language, the aesthete-baiting Gold merely refers to "that shallow clarity and tight little good taste that remind one of nothing so much as the conversation and practice of a veteran cocotte."

Today, Gold seems like the literary muscle of the Communist party, someone ready to enforce the standards of the gang on the independent artist. But in 1930 the attack looked different: Gold was a respected figure in the movement whose integrity was rarely questioned and whose book, *Jews Without Money*, exposed a side of American injustice. Wilder by contrast had recently made a great deal of money by presenting the agonies of materially comfortable people; he was also undeniably genteel—second-generation Yale, restrained in speech and manner, very much the child of the solid and enlightened professional class. Neither a rogue like Fitzgerald nor a manly adventurer like Hemingway, Wilder was a target for an adversary looking to make social style the criterion of literary worth. And finally, there is a certain cultural importance in Gold's remarks, especially if we gauge the American taste. Philip Rahv has distinguished between Paleface and Redskin American writers. The former, like Henry James, were analytic, polished, and ambivalent; the latter, like Walt Whitman, were freewheeling and undraped in their attitudes toward experience.[22] Wilder—clearly the former sort—is a writer who makes many readers think of Gold's "tight" good taste. That this characterization is crude does not prevent it from being potent.

During the 1930s Wilder turned to America for subject matter, but not in a way that pleased ideologues or made him a major reporter on the Depression. Wilder's America was a strange pastiche of elements—literary motifs, bits of comedy, echoes of European literature, ironic glimpses of the American character. *Heaven's My Destination*, conceived in 1932, was once thought to be a dutiful response to Gold's attack: concerned with a traveling textbook salesman and the ordinary people of the Midwest, the novel at first seems like a remorseful response to Gold's demands for social realism. Without any rancor, Wilder was later to comment that this view of his work was simply false.[23] While at Chicago he had been reading *Don Quixote:* his latest literary reaction was moral and cultural, not social and economic. He also told a *Paris Review* interviewer that the book was an attempt to come to terms with the pious didacticism of his upbringing.[24] As a literary and cultural response to Protestant stubbornness, the book is as satiric as Wilder ever gets—and in its anatomizing of its self-righteous

but likable protagonist, the novel is exceptionally witty
—or, as Edmund Wilson put it, "a Mozartian combination of lightness and grace with seriousness."[25]

While working on the book, Wilder came under
the influence of Gertrude Stein. A 1934 lectureship
at Chicago was her first American stay after years in
Paris—where, strangely enough, she had remained
staunchly American in her idioms, attitudes, and old-
fashioned Republican politics. Wilder, it seems, redis-
covered his country by listening to an expatriate who did
not feel at odds with the style of the American language
and the nature of American national aspirations. The two
writers became fast friends: Wilder's innately conservative nature and his gentlemanly manners made for
smooth relations with the touchy Stein. Wilder was always dutiful to masters, whether his father, his teachers,
or his literary predecessors. He read Stein's books with
care and wrote prefaces to them. Gilbert Harrison has
done the best reporting on Wilder's effusive responses
to this new mentor. Of *The Geographical History of the
United States* Wilder commented: "What a book. I
mean what a book! I've been living for a month with ever
increasing intensity on the conceptions of Human Nature and the Human Mind and on the relations of Masterpieces to their apparent subject matter." The distinction referred to between Human Nature and the Human
Mind became a central one in Wilder's life, a friend's
formulation of his own sense of man's situation: Human
Nature is a matter of identity, personality, and particularity. Wilder sought something beyond it, the Human
Mind's capacity to escape time and the stamp of the self
through art. The more playful part of Wilder, soon to
make its appearance in *The Merchant of Yonkers*, referred to Stein's complicated book this way: "Gertrude,
Alice, what a grand book. What an airplane ride. What a
quilting party, what a spelling bee."[26]

In 1935, he went to visit Stein and Alice B. Toklas

in the Haute Savoie. The effect of knowing Stein in Europe caused him to realize that he was

crazy about America, and you did that to me . . . my country 'tis of thee, I always knew I loved it, but I never knew I loved it like this. Every Childs' Restaurant, every shoe blacking parlor. I don't feel as though I ever had to leave it again. I was born into the best country in the world. Gertrude told me so.[27]

The substance of this outpouring takes on considerable meaning when we look forward in Wilder's career; most of the works ahead—*Our Town, The Merchant of Yonkers, The Skin of Our Teeth,* a large portion of *The Eighth Day* and *Theophilus North*—are set in America. Yet, the country that Wilder will create is like his outburst—a matter of ardors and impressions and a powerful attraction to an ideal rather than to a historical place.

Meanwhile, Wilder's life in the 1930s was congested with university commitments, public lecturing, and family responsibilities. He suffered a mild breakdown in 1935, a setback that required his leaving the university and, tired and troubled as he was, dashing to Europe. The problem seemed to be a career crisis combined with certain private burdens that aggravated his writing worries. Papa died in 1936 and "the protracted exasperating unloveable death"[28] left Wilder with a sense that he had not done enough for the solicitous parent. Soon after, Wilder was in Vienna paying a call on Freud. In the great man's study he had a chance to get another response to his work. Freud did not like *Heaven's My Destination,* both because of its religious concerns and what he considered the author's flippancy about the serious question of human illusions.[29] Freud also wanted Wilder to meet his daughter—hardly an inviting prospect for a man with Wilder's uncertainties about commitment. Seeing Freud made him think about the problems that originate in the family: "All we Wilders are as crazy as coots"[30] is a casual way of expressing the turmoil that resulted from the battle of values in his home. Altogether, the Vienna visit must have been an anxious occasion on which his problems converged. Wilder needed some release from the pain, constraint, and needling comments of family and critics. He also needed a way out of his "type" of novel—the delicately crafted work of sensibility and ironic distance.

"Why don't you write a play?" Norman Bel Geddes, the theater designer, suggested.[31] A full-length drama was an attractive project, yet a daunting undertaking for a writer who had not done a long dramatic work since his Yale days. *Our Town*—written very slowly and with great enthusiasm—was the response to the suggestion and the confrontation of his 1930s crisis. It inaugurated a playwriting period that proved successful until the early 1940s. The play brought with it deep personal satisfaction, public recognition, and a Pulitzer Prize. But new kinds of irritation also presented themselves.

Wilder broke out of his slump with "a little play with all the big subjects in it"—or "a big play with all the little things lovingly impressed into it." And yet the pleasure of creating a new kind of theatrical experience for American audiences—free of box set, conventional verisimilitude, and the other trappings of the naturalistic theater—was damaged by the business of working for the commercial stage. His director, Broadway wonder boy Jed Harris, was the next in the line of detractors who didn't like Wilder's language. "He fools around with the text alluding to his vast experience," Wilder wrote Edmund Wilson in a 1938 letter in which he ventilated about his problem with Harris. In shaping the play for production, Harris pressured Wilder into altering "my beautiful prose." "Prose doesn't play," the director insisted.[32] The changes, Wilder later maintained, made the play seem like a local-color piece. "Jed gyped me on the cosmic overtones." *Our Town*, one of the most sparely and brilliantly crafted plays of its time, was not destined for a dignified career on the American stage and screen: Wilder himself took part in the manhandling of the screenplay, complete with a happy ending; on television Frank Sinatra even got to play the Stage Manager.[33] Wilder's pliable nature certainly played a part in the erosion of his work's integrity.

But theater was his medium again. *The Merchant of Yonkers*, a farcical look at humanity's struggle for pleasure and joy, appeared in 1939. An adaptation of a work by the Austrian playwright Nestroy, which Wilder replanted in the New York of the 1880s, the play was the first version of *The Matchmaker* and the script on which *Hello, Dolly!* was eventually based. As it was metamorphosed during Wilder's lifetime, through his revisions and through the efforts of composer lyricist Jerry Herman in the musical comedy, the play lost its sharp critical edge and became just another commercial entertainment. The sly and playful spirit of the original version of *The Merchant of Yonkers* warmed Wilder up for his greatest comic work, *The Skin of Our Teeth*. *The Merchant* is a bridge between two plays about destiny, time, and endurance: it is the connective between the tragic vision of *Our Town* and the reconstitutive spirit of *The Skin of Our Teeth*.

In the late 1930s, Wilder began to give a good deal of time to writing about the ways in which he encountered literature and art. Now part of the public record of Wilder's achievement as a writer and intellectual, *The Journals of Thornton Wilder 1939–1961* offer a rich sampling of ideas and impressions of literature, philosophy, and the arts and an account—often cheerful, but sometimes distressed and frustrated—of the artist's works in progress.[34] His wide-ranging scholarly interests—motifs in Palestrina, the dating of Lope de Vega's plays, the text of *Finnegans Wake*, the defining qualities of classic American authors, techniques in Dickens, Stendhal, Cervantes, Thorstein Veblen's failings as a

thinker—make this document an extraordinary one, especially if one measures Wilder's explorations against
those of his contemporaries in America. As a playwright
and novelist, he was certainly equipped with curiosity
that no other peer could rival. And *The Journals* show
the process by which he enriched and transformed his
own stage and fictional plans through the use of other
writers' visions. Kafka, Kierkegaard, Genet, Sartre, the
philosophes, Mann, Boccaccio, the Greeks, Zen Bud-
dhism: his unfailing appetite for literature, art, and
thought takes the form of a delight in deriving—
typically, a passage about an author will tell about a motif that Wilder wanted for his own work. *The Journals*
chronicle these literary experiences for some twenty-two
years; true to Wilder's conservative, indeed mysteri-
ously evasive nature, they have very little to say about
personal problems, sexual attitudes, and the private
lives of the Wilders. During this period his sister Charlotte suffered a series of nervous breakdowns; in 1946 his
mother died; Thornton—if we are to credit Gilbert
Harrison's record of Wilder's erotic life—experienced
the pleasures and regrets of a number of relationships.
And yet these *Journals* pursue his cultural obsessions
with little reference to the drives and suffering that generally give shape to writers' notebooks. Wilder deplores
André Gide's self-absorption and accuses him of telling
an ersatz secret in his homosexual revelations. By contrast, Wilder felt he was revealing his true secret in describing his literary loves: more than anything available
to us, this record supplies the relevant environment of
Western literature and art that permeates his works. To
search out further new secrets from Wilder's life may
well make him a more understandable person; such a
search is unlikely to tell us much about the textures of
The Bridge of San Luis Rey or *Our Town*.

Before *The Skin* was produced in 1942, Wilder was
occupied with several nonliterary jobs—the latest exam-

ples of his tendency to follow Papa's advice about practical work. In 1941, before Pearl Harbor, he assumed a State Department position as a goodwill ambassador to several South American countries. The mission was a matter of cocktail hours, soirées, speeches, and readings —everything that could distract a writer from his work. When the war broke out, he volunteered and was accepted into Army Air Intelligence: he loved the immersion in the nonliterary and enjoyed "being pure instrument, however modestly, in a movement."[35] Here at least he had found an uncomplicated authority to submit himself to. He wrote little or nothing from 1942 to 1945.

During the war, there was a corrosive criticism gnawing at Wilder's reputation. *The Skin of Our Teeth* opened on Broadway in 1942 at a time when Captain Wilder had barely assumed his duties. On leaves, the author scuttled between his Washington post and New York rehearsals. Once again, the production—with Tallulah Bankhead playing the maid-seductress Sabina in a careening and uncontrolled style—was threatening to run off with the text and disappear into the realms of burlesque. Wilder's ironic collage of images and situations was in the hands of egomaniacs. But the worst part of the *Skin* experience came a month after the play opened to generally favorable reviews. The critics' axe swung again, this time in a *Saturday Review of Literature* article by two Joyce scholars, Joseph Campbell and Henry Morton Robinson. Wilder was accused of plagiarizing Joyce's *Finnegans Wake*.[36] Preposterous as the charge was, it did seem to connect with Wilder's special interests: for years he had been poring over Joyce's text—and he certainly did borrow several of Joyce's methods including conflation of time, mixing of images, cyclic patterning, and finding correspondences between the lives of ancient and modern man. But the accusation is the more outrageous for being insensitive to the nature of dramatic art: Joyce's work is wholly without the

page-to-page conflict and character-building that is the
playwright's contribution to literature. Wilder's play also
had its own humor, settings, and social vision. And if
Wilder was a literary thief, what was Joyce himself with
his quotations, echoes of other writers, Viconian plot,
and mythic parallels? Edmund Wilson came to Wilder's
defense: "Joyce is a great quarry, out of which a variety
of writers have been getting and will continue to get a
variety of different things; and Wilder is a genuine poet
with a form and imagination of his own who may find his
themes where he pleases without incurring the charge of
imitation."[37] Wilder himself offered the kind of sensible
generalization that explains the position of the highly literate writer: "Every story is consciously based upon
some other story in existence; it adds little increments or
manipulates it."[38]

Later on, Wilder commented that Campbell and
Robinson would derive *Junior Miss* from *Lady Chat-
terley's Lover*.[39] But no matter how reasonable and incisive the defenses were, the damage still remained. The
New York Drama Critics Circle passed over Wilder's
play and favored Sidney Kingsley's *The Patriots*, a conventional historical drama. When the Pulitzer Prize was
awarded to *The Skin*, it was not much comfort to an author who had been accused of dishonesty. Wilder may
also have felt the sting of leftist intellectuals speaking
through Mary McCarthy, their young tartaress: she
called the play a middlebrow sellout and apologia for
capitalism.[40] Wilder once wrote in his *Journals* that
Amos Wilder's confident children were all "notably well
removed from being impressed or depressed by the
evaluation of the neighbors"; the author had been taught
that negative critics were not fools, but neither were
they appropriate redirectors of our lives and talents.
Such an unpeevish attitude must have sustained him in
this period.

Except for *The Ides of March*, published in 1948,

and a few extraordinary plays produced in the early 1960s, the twenty years after the war were filled with forced work and false starts, strewn with abandoned projects, and occupied with the busy work of literature rather than the passion of creating. The attacks on the use of models struck at the roots of Wilder's art. Fortunately he did not abandon his intense involvement with past literature, but he did fall prey to a certain panic, depression, and miscalculation. When he worked on a drama like *The Alcestiad*, he failed to inform the Greek story with his own deft touch: the play was ponderous and reached the stage in Edinburgh in stillborn form. On the other hand, *The Ides of March* had the strange, technically odd quality of his 1920s novels: delicately melancholic, highly wrought, ironic, and charged by his old themes of mortality and the mystery of human suffering. Although it succeeds brilliantly as an evocation of the ancient Roman temper and an artfully plotted experimental work, the book was ignored by the intellectuals.

In the forties Wilder was working on a three-act play called *The Emporium*. Set in an American department store, the drama had its origins in Wilder's attraction to Franz Kafka's *The Castle*, particularly to the themes of mysterious human institutions and man's futile search for coherence. The *Journals* now tell us the full story—genesis, influences, struggles, frustrations, abandonment. Apparently Wilder wanted to combine the unsettling quality of Kafka's story with—it seems hard to believe—a Horatio Alger motif. About a young man who wants to "belong" to the labyrinthine world of a strange department store, the plot thread is complicated by Wilder's involvement with Kierkegaard's angst, Saint John of the Cross's "dark night of the soul," and his own ideas about transcendence. In the attempt to harmonize unharmonizeable elements, he only managed to tangle himself up for years: disillusioned with his own techniques in *Our Town* and *The Skin of Our Teeth*, he

sought a new kind of "originality" in his fusions. The result is a collection of pages with interesting motifs, prose
commentaries, and half-formulated plans.[41] Under the
weight of the abstract themes, Wilder's natural liveliness
and spontaneity evaporated. He became nervous, full of
self-doubt, unable to construct a resolution, unclear
about his protagonist's destiny. "You could repaper a
house with what I've thrown away,"[42] he remarked. The
writer who had handled his relationship with literary ancestors with such grace and success—who employed the
textures of Proust, Joyce, James, Cervantes, and Terence—was floundering with Kafka. The creative engine
that transformed others' motifs into Wilder's property
was stalled. The latest authority figure was an incubus
rather than an inspiration.

For a famous writer who has lost the visionary
gleam, there are always public enterprises. The most
enervating of these was Wilder's 1950 appointment as
Charles Eliot Norton lecturer in American literature at
Harvard; this academic plum turned out to be a source of
frustration. At first it seemed stimulating—filled with
parties, new research possibilities, great students. But
the obligation to publish lectures on classic American authors like Melville and Poe was hardly a minor responsibility. And, as Gilbert Harrison has suggested, Wilder's
mind was most at home with narrative forms, not with
exposition and argument.[43] Wilder loved to seek large
generalizations, but not in the form of essays. The Norton lectures hung over him for years, like some unpleas-
ant student task that must be completed. In the *Journals*
Wilder can be observed brooding on this work and its
difficulties—"the herd of obstacles in my path before I
can return to my rightful situation." Perhaps expository
writing was draining energy and turning him away from
symbols, images, and scenes—the proper concerns of
the imaginative writer. And yet, Wilder's naturally sanguine temperament made him think that speculations

about American literary culture—especially about the struggle between paternalism and liberty in the classic American works—might give shape to his own creative plans. In fact this tension between authority and freedom did emerge in his late work—particularly in the play *Childhood* and the massive novel *The Eighth Day*.

During the fifties there were other useful and futile digressions from the real business of writing. He tinkered with revisions of his works—*The Merchant of Yonkers,* a play whose title expressed the economic pressures of the thirties, emerged in a softened version as *The Matchmaker.* He pursued literary hobbies such as his interest in Lope de Vega. Dating the playwright's works became a kind of passion. He traveled too much, gave too many talks, and delivered too many ill-considered judgments. As a playwright and novelist whose work had a strong populist appeal from the thirties onward, Wilder had developed a sense of himself and the world that was distinctly egalitarian and at odds with the mandarinism and disillusionment of contemporaries like T. S. Eliot. A speech in Frankfurt took on the Eliotic disdain for the progressive spirit of our era: Wilder laced into aristocracies and paternalistic societies and their defenders. He cited the subjection of women, the brutalization of laboring children, and the downtrodden condition of working men in so-called golden ages of aristocracy and culture. The none-too-subtle approach of the sincere democrat—hardly what Mike Gold could have objected to—nevertheless earned Wilder further abuse. Eliot called the speech "sheer nonsense"; once again Wilder's devotion to masters—now Thomas Jefferson and Walt Whitman—produced yet another distressing reaction. This time, however, Wilder's lack of subtlety invited Eliot's dismissal.[44]

Honorary degrees poured in, but little distinguished work was finished in the 1950s. Amos Wilder,

the author's brother, speaks of Thornton's "total humanistic outreach" as it involves other things than writing
—"This artist's role included all such gregariousness, involvement, pedagogy, and missions."[45] Although a noble rationalization, this remark cannot really convince us
that Wilder was not frustrated and hampered by celebrity status as well as by his own self-indulgence and im-
patience with difficult work. Wilder even confessed to a
"vast accumulated self-discontent" about his desultory
work methods. Grand designs about a play cycle were
formed—the new title was to be "The Seven Ages of
Man." But only *Infancy* and *Childhood*, two fine, ironic
plays, were to be completed. The old freedom and imagination were on display in these little dramas, and also in
Someone from Assisi, but there was no evidence that
Wilder was entering a period of intense productivity. A
fascinating project called *The Sandusky Mystery Play*, a
small-town pageant that tried to experiment with stage
technique, is reminiscent of *Our Town* and the feeling
for the particularity of life evinced in that work. But the
play was dropped—a symbolic failure suggesting Wilder's disillusionment with his own best modes. "Maybe,
all can be saved yet," Wilder remarked in the *Journals*.
The record of publication and production does not support this optimism.

Wilder moved beyond this impasse and regained
his footing by returning to fiction. In 1963 he spent a
stretch of time in a small Arizona desert town, evidently
drying out from two decades of furious traveling, performing, and socializing. Cut off from theater friends,
cocktail hours, and the official duties of the man of letters, he produced ninety pages of a new manuscript; the
book was to be called *Anthracite*, and it was his most ambitious fictional undertaking in terms of theme and design. Set in southern Illinois, Hoboken, St. Kitts, and
South America, the novel dealt with the fortunes of a
man falsely accused of murder. Wilder—never a writer

involved with tight plots—was interested less in the mystery and more in the large patterns of endurance in the protagonist's life. Kierkegaard's "man of faith" was Wilder's latest paradigm of human survival. Like *The Bridge*, this new narrative was involved with the purpose and coherence, if any, in our world. The book was designed to discover a new bridge in its protagonist's faith. And, like *The Skin of Our Teeth*, it was about reconstitution and evolution.

Wilder earned little praise for this searching study of man's perdurability. *The Eighth Day* was acquired by the Book of the Month Club and earned money, but was either ignored or patronized by the New York intellectuals. *The New Republic* dismissed the book as meaningless. Stanley Kauffmann's review was especially damaging in that he ridiculed Wilder's lapses in style, his portentousness, and a tendency to substitute epigrams and sermons for characterizations. Even more serious were Kauffmann's general speculations about Wilder: recognizing Wilder's oddity and position as a "wanderer and observer," he nevertheless spoke of "the thinning of the artistic blood, the substitution of the literary cracker-barrel for ruthless vision."[46] The *New York Times* found Wilder condescending and old-fashioned. A critic like Denis Donoghue, whose skills had been honed on modernism, considered the book to be lacking in shape and purpose. Although Edmund Wilson commented in a letter that it was Wilder's best work, the encouragement was delayed. The only solid praise came from Malcolm Cowley, a man of Wilder's vintage and an appreciator of a fellow writer who didn't fit any "category."[47] He recognizd that Wilder's book—at once philosophical, sophisticated, and intensely European in its style and ambitions—was "untimely in a spectacular fashion," given the climate of America in 1967.

Wilder was understandably disappointed by the

generally cool reception of his strangely reflective novel, and changed styles and modes in his last work. *Theophilus North* is cast in an autobiographical mold and departs from the realistic manner of *The Eighth Day*; while the new book was fantastic, ironic, and charged by Wilder's cosmic sense, it was also somewhat bogged down by a combination of flat characterizations and nostalgia for the Newport of Wilder's youth. Never quite at his best when he used reminiscence, Wilder lapsed into certain cheery recollections of types and the ways in which his shrewd and amiable persona helped to straighten out the unhappy lives of Newport's socially important and humble citizens. In the end, Theophilus seemed almost to be playing the role of Dolly Levi.[48]

Wilder died in "the House the Bridge built" on December 7, 1975. While the honors piled up in the last decade, the creative satisfactions were meager when we measure his late work against the prose produced by Hemingway, Faulkner, and Fitzgerald in their last years. Nevertheless, Wilder did succeed in resisting the temptation to abandon his venturesome, outreaching idea of literature in favor of imitating his own successes, writing in one mode, or cultivating some familiar acreage. In his last novel he was overly caught up in his own fantasies: but the fact that he attempted yet another landscape and another style attests to his literary daring.

In spite of his range, depth, commitment to serious themes and to an arduous career of developing his multifaceted talent, Wilder still remains a stranger to most critics and intellectuals. In 1975 Malcolm Cowley wrote that the "ateliers (i.e., of the Upper West Side and Greenwich Village) have failed to discuss his work, and so, unfortunately, have most of our serious critics. In point of intelligent criticism, Wilder is the most neglected author of a brilliant generation."[49] Benjamin DeMott, a critic who labeled Wilder "an old-fashioned innovator," made a point similar to Cowley's in 1967 and also took shots at the tepid and unimaginative work of Wilder's friendly critics. Yet his own evaluation of Wilder—mostly a matter of saying that he represented an older America—did not suggest any new avenues for interpretation.[50] Even Francis Fergusson, a reasonably sympathetic major critic who did explore Wilder's dramatic art, was essentially puzzled about Wilder's contribution—and willing to refer to his special place (between "the Great Books and Paris" and the commercial world of entertainment) as "no man's land."[51] This explanation of Wilder's neglect and shortcoming needs to be qualified: interesting as it is, it does not account for enough, and it sells Wilder short by once again making him sound like a middlebrow compromiser. The identity that Wilder established was that of the writer who feels more comfortable with exploration than with settlement. In his appetite for change and experiment, for taking chances and risking failure, we will find his gifts as a novelist and playwright and his courage as a man.

2

Isolation in Wilder's Foreign Novels

The Cabala, The Bridge of San Luis Rey, and *The Woman of Andros* are a part of the literature of isolation and chaos that gave expression to early twentieth-century pressures. Wilder absorbed the spirit of his age and took his place as a distinguished supporting artist in the struggle to express the disorder and sense of disintegration that also haunted the late James, the young Hemingway, and the Eliot of "Prufrock" and *The Waste Land*. Despite his use of fabricated historical settings, his first three novels are "in our time" because they focus on damaged selves and short-circuited relationships. In an elegant prose that was modern without being either difficult or colloquial, Wilder studied people who were falling apart. His vulnerable and perishing men and women live in the same emotional territory as modern fiction's most famous agonized protagonists. Like Proust's Swann, Eliot's Prufrock, James's Strether, and Hemingway's Jake Barnes and Nick Adams, Wilder's best characters engage us because of their peculiarly modern malaise and exhaustion. Whether he located his narratives in eighteenth-century Peru, twentieth-century Rome, or Hellenistic Greece, he trained his sights on injured identities rather than on conventional story lines.

No old-fashioned writer in the genteel tradition of the late nineteenth century could have writen *The Cab-*

ala. The wit and irony, ingenuity of craftsmanship, and bleakness of coloration make it a distinct, if not totally successful, modern novel. Sometimes dismissed as a priggish or puritanical study of a young American's Roman sojourn, the book is confused with "refined" novels of European holidays; but the excellence of its texture and design—shaped to reveal the failures of a whole class of people—becomes apparent to the reader who is willing to grant Wilder his own artistic terms.

The narrative concerns the arrival of two young Americans in Rome, and the entrance of the narrator-protagonist into the precious, fragile, and demented lives of the Cabala members, a group of aristocratic Europeans and Americans who live off enormous incomes and only for their dreams and illusions. Samuele, a classicist and the teller of the story, is traveling with the pedantic young Puritan James Blair, a Harvard-trained student of antiquities whose brain teems with useless facts and whose heart is as arid and humanly useless as his intellect. Blair, presently "bent on transferring the body of Greek mythology to the screen" as archaelogical advisor to a film studio, offers our narrator Samuele the amusing idea of finding out about the folkways of the Cabala: as patricians, the Cabala people are curiosities of the human species whose lives are "so powerful and exclusive that all these Romans refer to them with bated breath." They intrigue in politics and the church, espouse forgotten or lost causes, and conduct their lives within "a pocket of archaic time." Like Proust's Baron de Charlus, who made old-fashioned expressions seem chic and clever, they offer an ultra-conservatism and eccentricity that seem fascinating to curious American outsiders.

The book, which is divided into five parts, is Samuele's series of encounters with a world within the modern world, an often wild and pathetic wasteland of shattered fantasies. "First Encounters" takes him across the Campagna in a train with Blair. During the short trip, there "was a wind that seemed to rise from the fields and descend upon us in a long Vergilian sigh." A sigh of futility, Samuele discovers, pervades the life of Miss Grier, the American leader of the international set and the descendant of a Dutch railroad magnate. A conduit of Cabala information, she tries to fill "the moneyed emptiness of her days" with schemes to help her friends —and with desperate attempts to keep her visitors amused with salons and all-night musicales. Her German band-in-residence and her Fortuny gowns smack of Wilder's close reading of Proust.[1] In this atmosphere, Samuele meets one of the novel's principal oddities —the "high Merovingian maiden" Marie-Astrée Luce de Monfontaine, a preposterous woman who wants an ecumenical council to proclaim officially the divine right of kings—and learns about other members like the witty Cardinal Vaini and the beautiful Alix, Princess D'Espoli. In a digressive conclusion to the chapter that at first seem irrelevant to a narrative about an exclusive social group, Samuele and Blair walk at evening near the Spanish Steps and pay a call on a dying poet—obviously patterned on Keats—who suffers because of his aborted career and recognizes that his name is "writ in water." Readers who find this touch gratuitous or pretentious should look back to the futility already presented in Chapter 1, and forward to Wilder's other victims. The facricating mind in *The Cabala,* whether scheming for causes or writing poems, cannot brave time and decay.

"Book Two: Marcantonio" is about another kind of destruction. La Duchessa D'Aquilanera, a Colonna married to a Tuscan with a thirteenth-century title, appears to our witty narrator as "a short, black-faced woman with two aristocratic wens on the left slope of her nose, yellow, dirty hands covered with paste emeralds (an allusion to her Portuguese claims; she was archduchess of Brazil, if Brazil had only remained Portuguese)." She puts before Samuele the problem of her son Marcan-

tonio, a sports-car-driving libertine of sixteen who is
ruining his chances for a good marriage by not settling
down after "his five or six little affairs." Samuele, a solid
son of New England, is shocked and agrees to become
enlisted as a combination sports coach and brotherly
advisor to the young rake. The chapter introduces the
suave and brilliant Cardinal Vaini, a worldly and world-
weary prelate who knows the boy and slyly asks Samuele
to keep him "quiet" for a while. The strategic quality in
the Cardinal's idea of virtue is another shock to an American. So is the Cardinal's simple declaration that "we are
in the world." "Never try to do anything against the bent
of human nature" is the morality of the Cardinal. "I came
from a colony guided by exactly the opposite principle,"
Samuele reflects. He soon takes on the task of handling
Marcantonio, but ironically forgets his own sound observation. Adapting the central situation of Henry James's
The Ambassadors—an older man of puritanical tenden-
cies sent to redeem a young pleasure lover—Wilder dis-
patches Samuele on his mission: but unlike James's
novel about a Puritan's awakening, Wilder's chapter is
about the disaster of moral impositions.[2] Samuele gives
the boy a dose of New England fire and brimstone,
destabilizes his already fragile mind, and causes him—
in an overly contrived scene of sin and self-hatred—to
kill himself. Transatlantic impulses—the European's
search for pleasure, the American's desire for righteousness—collide. But Wilder's presentation of the collision
is by no means as interesting as his cameo portraits.

"Book Three: Alix" continues to explore the disaster
of love. This time the victim is a vibrant egocentric
blonde princess whose marriage is loveless and whose
life consists of pathetic attempts to attract young Anglo-
Saxons like Blair. The section charts her harmless but ridiculous strategies, her desperation, and eventual failure. Blair—another one of her "cool, impersonal,
learned, or athletic Northerners"—is Wilder's blind and

desiccated embodiment of the puritanical American: unlike the Puritan Samuele, he cannot even see what is
around him or feel the agony of others. A rather prissy
pursuer of beauty in classical art and literature, he cannot perceive value in the modern Rome that he moves
in: a beautiful woman's face is so many folds and pores;
only an ancient map or text can hold his attention. Alix's
unrequited passion is drawn out in a manner reminiscent of Proust's treatment of the Swann-Odette affair in
Swann's Way: Wilder, of course, makes the tormented
lover a woman; he also, unfortunately, makes her
slightly silly and tedious. The ending of the section—a
scene in which Alix, restored to social life in the Cabala
after a disappearance, hears the unresponsive Blair
praised—shows her as she melodramatically faints "with
a happy smile upon her face." The opportunity to por-
tray a tragically thwarted woman is lost—most obviously
because Alix is a case rather than a fully developed character.

"Book Four: Astrée Luce and the Cardinal" is, along
with the opening chapter, the best-sustained piece of
writing in the book. Wilder's considerable gift for irony
is evident as he shows another collision—this time not a
matter of Eros thwarted or denied, but a wonderfully
ludicrous confrontation between wit and obtuseness,
sophistication and complete naïveté. Not only are the
erotic energies of Cabala members derailed by their
defects of temperament; their limited intellects are also
warped by the isolation of patrician Rome. Astrée Luce
is like some ridiculous figure built along the lines of
Bergson's idea of comedy as human rigidity: we laugh at
this woman who pursues her absurd idea of divine right
of kings just as we laugh at the mechanical inflexibility of
a silent-film comic actor. Her dense, innocent mind is
also guided by a simplistic conception of Christian faith
and the efficacy of prayer: like a little child, she feels that
God bargains with man. True to the structure of the

other two chapters—in each a character is destroyed by
seeing that his or her vision is fruitless in light of the nature of others' desires and visions—Astrée presents her
cherished nonsense to the Cardinal and is devastated by
his corrosive, cerebral reactions. The first of Wilder's
ironic spectators, an onlooker like Uncle Pio in *The
Bridge* and the stage manager in *Our Town,* the Cardinal is a philosophical observer who has endured pain and
the jealousy of his mediocre fellow priests, often suffered
fools, and yet retained his mental poise and style. Like
Samuele with Marcantonio, however, he does not have
the gift of human tact—he provokes the poor cracked
believer with his own skepticism, and she attempts to
shoot him. While he is unharmed, he is nevertheless
awakened to the crime of his own jaded nature: he once
was a man of faith who had converted many souls in
China; he is now a cynical old man who disdains the
modern world and who also cannot rekindle the faith of
his youth. Through this recognition, he ironically rises
above the sophistication that Wilder has made so fascinating in the course of the book: worldly wisdom is displaced by "a state of hope." The Cardinal and his friend
Astrée—through messages carried by Samuele—are
reconciled.

The final chapter, "The Dusk of the Gods," is a series of Samuele's musings as he is about to leave Rome.
Miss Grier reveals the final "secret" of the Cabala: the
old gods are still in the city and their new forms are
those of the Cardinal and Alix and the others—latter-
day pale incarnations of what was once great.[3] But eventually even gods die: "Finally tired out with the cult of
themselves they give in. They go over. They renounce
themselves." Wilder's narrator leaves the cult of self-
absorption and, as he sails from the Bay of Naples, in-
vokes Virgil and asks for guidance. Is he wrong to leave
Rome? The pretentious, ponderous exchange between
poet and traveler is an early distillation of Wilder's

themes of blindness and illusion. Virgil denounces the kind of vanity and pathetic illusion that Samuele has seen among the Cabala members. Rome and its patrician dreams and obsessions are not eternal.

Seek out some city that is young. The secret is to make a city, not to rest in it. When you have found one, drink in the illusion that she too is eternal.

No sooner does the poet exhort the narrator to be creative, than he destroys the substance of human endeavor with the word "illusion." Our life—like that of the Cabalists—is really no more than a displacement of an old illusion with a new one. Even Samuele, a citizen of the New World, en route to "the shelf of Manhattan," cannot transcend the pathetic limitations of human nature; the spirit of Virgil delivers this pronouncement:

All your thoughts are guesses, all your body is shaken with breath, all your senses are infirm, and your mind ever full of the fumes of one passion or another. Oh, what a misery to be a man.

While the ship's engines pound "eagerly" toward the "greatest of all cities," the American heart of the protagonist is left with its burden. Hardly any great breakthrough in the understanding of human nature, this didactic and windy ending—and much of the melodramatic plot material about the Cabalists—is unlikely to stand up as an important artistic vision. The book's interest lies in a few character portraits, its exquisite brief descriptions, and its complex relationship to modernism.

Wilder's first novel is an echo chamber of the themes, motifs, and strategies of twentieth-century literature. By no means a distinguished work, it is nevertheless a young writer's first fictional attempt to join the company of the Olympian talents who flourished between 1900 and 1945. Of the older generation of modernists, Henry James certainly looms large in Wilder's narrative. The central theme of *The Cabala*—the unrealized life, the forms of inhibition and inadequacy that block vital experience—is the focus of James's short story "The Beast in the Jungle." Each of Wilder's people awaits some rare, special kind of personal fulfillment. Like James's wintry character Marcher, each is incapable of making an ordinary discovery about human beings that will be a release from the prison of rare dreams and illusions. The Cabalists are encased in their specialness, and their sense of the world stands in apposition to Marcher's sense that he is on the brink of discovering some extraordinary destiny for himself. As noted, *The Cabala* also echoes the motifs of James's *The Ambassadors*: it is about a Puritan's encounters with European culture, standards of morality, and aesthetics. Wilder's Samuele, like James's Lambert Strether, is discovering what James called "a civilization more subtle": although we hear nothing about his American hometown—as we do about Strether's native Woolett, a New England mill town—we do see Samuele judging Alix and the Cardinal by the standards of Puritanism. The Cardinal's acknowledgment of human biological nature and of human weakness is at first as stunning a blow to Samuele's consciousness as is the idea of joy and pleasure to Strether.

But while James's novel is about discovering Europe too late, Wilder's book is about rising above a civilization that has become stifling in its manners, precious in its forms, and dangerous rather than nurturing. That Wilder wrote in 1926 and James wrote in 1903 should not be forgotten as we trace how awakening American Puritan protagonists looked at the Europe experience: the First World War destroyed an empire, irreparably damaged the social structure of Europe, and supplied the writers of the 1920s with a ready-made theme that became the grand idea of modernist art—dissolution.

Wilder takes some of James's materials—the Puritan's recognitions, the beauty of European manners, the idea of pleasure—but dissolves them in his own essentially tragic postwar vision. Written in the same decade as Oswald Spengler's *Decline of the West, The Cabala* is informed by a pessimism about aspirations, ideals, and enduring values of civilization. The representatives of Europe are two cracked women, a suicide, and a faithless cardinal.

The physical descriptions of the characters are another way that Wilder has of registering his theme of decline. At once humorous and deeply ironic, the images are no more used for purposes of conventional social satire than Eliot's images in "Prufrock" or *The Waste Land*. They express the author's spiritual awareness and feelings of distaste for his crumbling civilization. Wilder, like Eliot, has his protagonist moving in pretentiously cultured settings: while Prufrock is in a room where "the women come and go/Talking of Michelangelo," Samuele is also among the culture vultures, like Miss Grier:

She paid a group of singers from the Lateran choir to sing her endless Palestrina. She became prodigiously learned. Harold Bauer would listen meekly to her directions on phrasing Bach —he averred that she had the only truly contrapuntal ear of the age—and the Florzaleys acceded to her request to take certain pages of Loeffler a little slower.

When Wilder gives his attention to the tourists pouring into Rome, he is not quite so nasty as Eliot in "Burbank with a Baedecker, Bleistein with a Cigar," but the ironic impulse behind his description of the types is the same: vulgarity and triviality flood Wilder's Italy just as they invade Eliot's Venice. There are three Italian Americans on the train to Rome . . .

returning to their homes in some Apennine village after twenty years of trade in fruit and jewelry on upper Broadway. They had invested their savings in the diamonds on their fingers . . . one foresaw their parents staring at them, unable to understand the change whereby their sons had lost the charm the Italian soil bestows on the humblest of its children, noting only that they have come back with bulbous features, employing barbarous idioms and bereft forever of the witty psychological intuition of their race.

On the train there are also army officers compared to insects, Oxford students on a walking tour who are missing the beauty of walking across the Campagna, a Japanese businessman preoccupied with a stamp collection. "Such a company as Rome receives ten times a day, and still remains Rome." Later on, Mr. Frederick Perkins of Detroit, a culture-seeking invader who has pestered our narrator for an entrance into the Duchess D'Aquilanera's villa, finally brings to bear "all his American determination" and scales the garden wall. The seeker of the picturesque finds the villa "at its most characteristic"—with "a dead prince among the rose bushes."

Wilder's ironic characterization is most effective when he uses the aged Cardinal as a kind of intellectual and emotional distillation of European decline, self-absorption, and exhaustion. This elegant priest had a spectacular career as a student with the Jesuits; he capped his studies with a thesis "of unparalleled brilliance and futility" on the forty-two cases in which suicide is permissible. After rejecting advancement in Italy, he had a period of fabulous success as a missionary in China—effecting conversions, syncretizing Christianity with Chinese customs, building a great cathedral. On his return to Italy, however, he withdrew from society: a contempt for his fellow men caused him to retire to a villa, spend his time gardening, reading, and tending his pet rabbits. Piles of classic and modern books—Spengler, Freud, Montaigne—lie on his outdoor study table, but no writing is ever done. The old man refers to modern literature as "ordure"—and concedes that he could write something to surpass the work of his contemporaries, but "a Montaigne, a Machiavelli . . . a . . . Swift, I will never be." He seems to sink with the weight of the past, and his intellect—certainly a fine-tuned instrument capable of discerning the mediocrity and naïveté of his colleagues and his Cabala friends—is nevertheless incapable of releasing him from cynicism and despair. Wilder's early attempt to grapple with the limitations of the rational mind, the Cardinal is an eloquent and sad representation of modern blindness: unable for most of the book to see the neediness of a simple-minded woman, he is also incapable of identifying his own despair until it is too late to overcome it and live. Mired in his own fruitless exquisiteness—sitting talking to Samuele on one occasion in "a fine shadow"—he has a mind that can command but that has lost its direction through closing the portals that admit the reality of others' existences. In his letters,

always from the first sentence he foresaw his last and always like a movement from Mozart's chamber music the whole unit lay under one spirit and the perfection of the details played handmaid to the perfection of the form.

The end of his chapter makes this quotation very ironic in that a moment's realization about Astrée's pain causes him to awaken to the reality of someone else's world: it spoils the Mozartian unity of his life.

The Cabala is a novel about what might have been: this thematic line—traced out in a city that has only weary people in it—is certainly no leftover concern from the literary past, yet it is not pursued without lapses in plot and characterization. Hemingway's Jake in *The Sun Also Rises*, sitting with Lady Brett and thinking of how it could have been, Eliot's Prufrock, wondering if he should dare to eat a peach, James's Strether, almost encountering the full sensuousness of Europe: these three characters are more skillfully created than Wilder's people, but they are located in the same world of futility and desolation. *The Cabala* also falters because of its fairly frequent descents into melodrama and its essentially unsatisfactory central character-narrator. The book stages too many "scenes"—Marcantonio's suicide, Alix's faint, Astrée's mad murder attempt—and what is achieved in symmetry through the recurrences of these outbreaks is lost in verisimilitude. It furthermore seems that Samuele is taking a tour of Roman neurotic spectacles rather than living a life of his own. The onlooker, of course, is one of modern literature's familiar figures. But this observer, while often capable of witty remarks, seems unburdened with any pressing conflict of his own or any reasons other than passing time for doing what he does among *The Cabala*'s people. His obvious limitations are left hanging in midair.[4] While Wilder directs us toward his puritanical nature, he does not make him confront himself. Samuele also seems to be a directionless loiterer rather than a center of consciousness. Because of this unresolved, shadowy portraiture in its central figure, the novel seem glued together by coincidences rather than welded by a controlling intellect.

The Bridge of San Luis Rey emerges from this world of decline and exhaustion: although it begins with another group of people who are frustrated by weakness and social destiny, it struggles to rise above the disasters of the modern world into a sustaining, if not always entirely clear, spirituality. While the Cabala members are made to thrash around in their own frustrations, the characters of *The Bridge* are offered certain epiphanies before they die. Wilder, the godlike omniscient author, doles out insights to a group of eighteenth-century Peruvian people who are initially caught in troubles that resemble those of Alix, the Cardinal, and the others. But the second novel is about the bridge of love that looms up paradoxically from human misery; Wilder's first book

is throughout controlled by the idea of an enclosing social circle and isolation.

The shape of *The Bridge* bears a considerable re-
semblance to that of *The Cabala;* both works are episodic, divided into chapters that focus on individual
characters. While the first novel practices this technique
of character representation, the second employs it in a
fully realized work of art. Wilder's failure with the
protagonist in *The Cabala* is overcome in *The Bridge*
through an intricate kind of distancing, a strategy of Chinese boxes that removes the narrator from the action.
Using the narrator as an omniscient commentator is, of
course, an old-fashioned device: but Wilder has his narrative voice commenting on another observer of the
book's events—one Brother Juniper, a devout and na-
ively philosophical Franciscan whose researches into the
lives of the characters become a level of meaning in
themselves. Then, of course, there are the characters'
own words and actions. Like the reader of Conrad's
"Heart of Darkness," the reader of *The Bridge* must
move from Wilder, the narrator, to another commentator to the central subjects of the story. The judgments
Wilder makes about all the characters are problematic
because two levels of reality interfere with the reader
and character. This strategy is much more engrossing
than the concerns of the shadowy Samuele in *The Cabala*. Wilder, if nothing else, has deflected attention from
the self of his narrator and thrown the emphasis on his
new group and the problems involved with understanding their fates. Through a sleight of hand he escapes having to examine his observer/narrator. The trick works
well in *The Bridge*, but Wilder's lifelong tendency to
evade the obligations of analyzing a protagonist have
strange consequences in later novels, especially in *The
Eighth Day* and *Theophilus North*.

The plot of *The Bridge* is no less ingenious than the
shaping of point of view. Essentially a disaster book, *The*

Bridge as a story is the ancestor of popular fictions about how people have led their lives and come to their ends on the same day. The device in itself seems cheap, but the interlocking character portraits and the destinies of the people are handled with a strangely effective blend of irony, deep emotion, and style. The accident of the narrative occurs on July 12, 1714, in Lima; an osier bridge built a century before by the Incas collapses, and five travelers crossing the bridge perish. Part One, "Perhaps an Accident," recounts how a certain Brother Juniper witnessed the accident, responded to the teleological dimension of the event, tried to prove that it was providential, and took six years to write a book which "was publicly burned on a beautiful spring morning in the great square." The narrator, who claims to know "so much more," equivocates with us by suggesting both the pagan and Christian interpretations of this disaster: human beings are like flies to wanton boys, and they are the sparrows whose falls are known to God.

Starting with these mysteries, Wilder devotes the rest of the book to the mysteries of the self. First there is "The Marquesa De Montemayor," a section involved with exploring the secret of the old, drunken woman who many years before married a ruined nobleman and had a child by him, Dona Clara. The focus of the chapter is the mother-daughter estrangement: although the Marquesa, another of Wilder's obsessive, emotionally needy characters, directs all her attentions on the young woman, including her great literary gifts, the girl is coldly indifferent and anxious to get away from this tyrant of love by going to Spain with her husband. The mother pursues her in eloquent letters, devotes her days to begging for love by mail, and eventually becomes one of the more ridiculous spectacles of Lima—so much so that a fiery young actress named Perichole, the great talent of the Lima stage, does a parodic bit of material one night that mocks the old woman. The Marquesa, en-

closed in her obsession, doesn't take offense. She cannot
see the insult any more than she can see the situation of
her young companion Pepita, a girl raised in a convent
and given as a maidservant to the old woman by the Abbess Maria del Pilar. Pepita, a morbidly obedient child,
has been taken from a place where she hoped to continue the work of her philanthropic Abbess. She serves
the Marquesa only out of duty: the climax and conclusion of this relationship comes when the Marquesa discovers, through an unfinished letter written by the girl,
that her young companion yearns for the company and
esteem of her former mentor. Life with the Marquesa
has been one long act of endurance and bravery. The
Marquesa—always eloquent on paper, often witty in the
midst of her pleading—takes up her pen and writes "her
first letter, her first stumbling misspelled letter in courage." She finishes and goes out to look "at the great tier
of stars above the Andes." The next day—when she has
already vowed to begin again after this recognition of another's being—she falls with Pepita from the bridge.

"Part Three: Esteban" is about twin brothers who
have been reared by the Madre Maria del Pilar. Manuel
and Esteban are inseparable: they live together, work
together, and even have a private language that shuts
out the world. However, their love for each other is disturbed by Manuel's attraction for the actress Perichole.
The illiterate woman seeks Manuel out to have letters
written; the young man subtly changes in his attitude toward his beloved brother as his attraction for the woman
grows. Esteban thus "discovered that secret from which
one never quite recovers, that even in the most perfect
love one person loves less profoundly than the other."[5]
When Manuel has an accident that injures his leg, he de-
velops an infection and finally falls into a delirium. In his
ravings, he curses his brother for coming between him
and the Perichole. Esteban—like the Marquesa—
discovers the truth of another's life. The brother dies,

and Esteban is left with his guilt, his damaged love, and his longing to die. Captain Alvarado, a seaman who has spent his own life running from grief, befriends him and offers a voyage. Just when Esteban is setting off with him, they fall from the collapsing bridge.

In "Part Four: Uncle Pio," Wilder's victim of love is also his most sophisticated and interesting character. Unlike the crazed Marquesa or the simple Esteban, Uncle Pio has a highly developed consciousness and a varied, rounded nature. A distillation of worldly knowledge and experience not unlike the Cardinal in *The Cabala*, Pio is nevertheless something more: a player of roles, a protean man who has lived by his wits as spy, pimp, agent provocateur, errand boy, animal trainer, acting coach, drama connoisseur. His latest role is that of man of all work for the Perichole: he reads to this illiterate, cares for her, and shapes her into a Lima celebrity. Once a cheap café performer, she now has been polished and transformed by this cultivated man with "his passion for overseeing the lives of others, his worship of beautiful women, and his admiration for the treasures of Spanish literature." After Pio has created Perichole (alias Camila), he yearns to perfect his work—to make her great enough for the Spanish stage and equal to his own vision. Vulgarian that she is, she pursues affairs and leaves the stage altogether to take up the role of great society lady. Living in a villa in the mountains, she removes herself from her past. A spectacle of a different kind from the Marquesa, she parades around in jewels and plumes and attempts to intimidate the local dowagers because she is the mistress of the Viceroy. All Pio's work has seemingly come to nothing; she breaks with her old friend and with the ideal of art he has established for her. After she contracts smallpox, she cuts herself off completely from society, believing that her life is contained in her facial beauty. Uncle Pio attempts to see her and is violently rebuffed. He wants some token of gratitude and asks her to let him educate her little son Jaime, a sickly child fathered by the Viceroy. After getting the mother's consent, Pio and the boy go off together and perish on the bridge.

"Perhaps an Intention" is the quiet, but highly ironic conclusion to the novel: as the last panel in this composition about disaster, it might have been expected that the chapter would have revealed Wilder's attitude toward chance and providence. But it is Brother Juniper, not Wilder's narrator, who plunges himself into speculation and writes a book. The good Franciscan "thought he saw in the same accident, the wicked visited by destruction and the good called early to Heaven." Our narrator goes through Juniper's calculations about good and bad people, useful and useless men and women. The tables that the man assembles prove almost nothing; the details of lives yield little; personal interviews with intimates of the victims yield less. For his researches Brother Juniper is burned in the public square. Like the Marquesa, Esteban, and Pio, he becomes another victim whose love—in this case, of divine order —is not understood. Wilder's narrator observes a village woman "Nina (Goodness 2, Piety 5, Usefulness 10)" watching the "congenial flames." To compound the irony, Wilder uses a narrator who has read much more than Juniper, who knows the hearts of the victims through letters and books unavailable to the Brother —but who still knows nothing. At the conclusion of the novel, the Marquesa's daughter comes back to Peru and expresses remorse; the Perichole does the same. But the narrator remains silent as the Abbess, the most perceptive reader of the disaster, reflects on death, forgetfulness—and "all those impulses of love" that cannot be killed by death or loss of memory. "There is a land of the living and a land of the dead and the bridge is love, the only survival, the only meaning." A fallen bridge provides the metaphor for the spiritual connection that ironically has nothing to do with details, calculations, ideas of Providence, or fears of chaos.

These "impulses of love" that connect the two realms of being are not created without the payment of a terrible price. Wilder leaves the reader to ponder the design and meaning of the book—the mingling of pain and joy, aggression and devotion, blindness and insight. People in this novel hurt each other, almost without knowing it: they live oblivious of friends, parents, and lovers. Dona Clara injures the Marquesa who in turn neglects Pepita. Manuel doesn't realize what he has done to his brother; the Perichole, of course, uses Pio only to discard him; she captivates Esteban without even caring. This network of casual brutality is Wilder's second vision of how life is blighted by neurotic obsession and willful neglect. Anticipating his existentialist attack on human blindness in two later novels—*The Ides of March* and *The Eighth Day*—*The Bridge* presents us with people who direct their attention at everything but the truth of their situations. The Marquesa is a human being, not a professional mother; Perichole is not a great lady, but rather a created, artificial identity; Pio is a man of many talents, not an errand boy for an egomaniac. Even Brother Juniper has lost himself in pursuit of his idea of Providence. But in the process of destroying themselves, the characters have all generated intense emotion: whether victims who realize, or survivors who transcend egoism, they endure, for Wilder, as emblems of the reality of feeling. The price, of course, has been suffering for all and death for six.

Another twentieth-century writer who dealt with the disasters of involvement and the bridges that the creative mind can construct in order to create meaning is, of course, Marcel Proust. Edmund Wilson has identified Proust's theme of love between emotional unequals, between the gentle and the cruel, as one of Wilder's key

motifs.[6] The theme is embodied by pairs of characters
in *Remembrance of Things Past* and in Wilder by Pio/
Perichole, the Marquesa/Dona Clara, and Esteban/
Manuel. In addition, Proust and the early Wilder both
have a sense of injury and alienation that may well be
caused in part by their homosexuality: the betrayals in
Remembrance of Things Past become much more than
instances of ordinary infidelity—Proust's narrator, for
example, lives in a shadowy world where love from
Albertine seems like some menacing, teasing, malevo-
lent force; Marcel's description is an almost cosmic vision of the world of feeling gone wrong. Wilder too is
involved with the generalized dissolution of love and
loyalty. His sensitive victims seem to be destroyed by
some ugly, antiromantic conspiracy carried out by brutal
tormentors. Equally important are certain odd details
and overriding affinities in these loves that show how
Wilder must have known Proust's work intimately.
Proust's Swann cries out:

To think that I have wasted years of my life, that I have longed
for death, that the greatest love that I have ever known has
been for a woman who did not please me, who was not in my
style!

Wilder's Uncle Pio is angry at the Perichole—his
cleaned-up Protestant version of Proust's designing
courtesan—because she has not attained his level of devotion to the theater and to the Spanish language. She is
also a strange spectacle to him because, like Proust's
Odette, she continues to regard people as objects and
love as a strategy. Both Uncle Pio and Charles Swann
are connoisseurs, men of culture and fine aesthetic sensibility. Proust very significantly has his protagonist
evaluating Odette by comparing her features to those of
women in Renaissance drawings and paintings. Pio's favored art form is poetic drama—and the Perichole is

measured severely against the greatness that could ide-
ally be attained in a performance of Calderón.

Wilder's "bridge" metaphor is ultimately his form of
compensation for the "cruel malady of love" on earth.
Proust, of course, has a far more complex and majestic
return on the investment of his suffering—a book with
seven volumes. But the desire to rise above the chaos of
human aggressions and illusions that Wilder presents in
The Bridge is charged with Proust's bravery, reverence
for created works, and desire to emulate masters: just as
the pages of *Remembrance of Things Past* are inlaid with
descriptions of art works against which Proust judges the
world of events, Wilder's book also has its artist figures
who stand up to the ravages of time by creating words
and images. The Marquesa—scorned in her time like
Proust's composer—creates a monument of Spanish
epistolary literature out of her neurosis. Although the
conditions of her existence involve neglect and humiliation, the letters that she composed reach across the cen-
turies and have become a standard for many Spanish
schoolboys. Uncle Pio's devotion to language has also
been an act of resistance against the sordid terms of his
life: the former street character, "a soiled pack of cards,"
as the Marquesa calls him, has risen above the climate of
Lima life through his obsession with "the lordly conversation" of Calderón. Pio's world is one in which the artist tortures himself in his attempt to transcend his
weakness and the indifference of his society. Although
Thornton Wilder presents his vision of the ideal realm of
art in terms that are less subtle psychologically than
Proust's sustained act of memory and reconstitution, he
nevertheless adapts the seminal conception of *Remembrance of Things Past*—faith in a realm of beauty and order that can be captured in words:

We come from a world where we have known incredible standards of excellence, and we dimly remember beauties which

we have not seized again; and we go back to that world. Uncle Pio and Camila Perichole were tormenting themselves in an effort to establish in Peru the standards of the theaters in some Heaven whither Calderón had preceded them. The public for which masterpieces are intended is not on this earth.

Wilder's tragic sense—certainly not a view of the errors and limitations of heroic people—is a vision of callousness in human relationships and the ravages of time. His chapters are not so much about the disaster of a fallen bridge as about the personal traumas, ridiculous, sometimes poignant, of five people, and, of course, of Brother Juniper. Each has been trapped in a kind of love that can only yield pain. Wilder, like Proust, is rather masochistic in his ability to find meaning and even joy in their lives of self-laceration. His book is firmly planted in the soil of emotional futility; it miraculously—almost too miraculously—rises to an affirmation about "impulses" of human love. The sleight of hand that has the Abbess saying that "the bridge is love" is of course in keeping with the design of the novel: she too has suffered greatly for her devotion to her hospital; she is discounted in the eighteenth century as a mere woman; she has lost her best worker. Her testimony at the end carries weight. Wilder, however, has preceded her affirmation with one too many realizations: his clumsy and sentimental denouement, with Dona Clara seeing her loss and Perichole doing the same, is like some last-minute rush to recognition. An exquisitely designed book is marred by too much neat remorse. Wilder betrays his own tragic vision by allowing it to degenerate into the Perichole's remark, "I am a sinner." In this Wilder loses the impact of the wrenching pain and chaos that he has shown us. It even looks dangerously as if everything might have been for the best in this world of sad cases.

Fortunately, he does not leave himself with these easy resolutions. The other dimension of the novel's tragedy, the reality of time and death and memory, looms at the conclusion. The Abbess thinks that,

almost no one remembers Esteban and Pepita, but myself. Camila alone remembers her Uncle Pio and her son; this woman, her mother. But soon we shall die and all the memory of those five will have left the earth, and we ourselves shall be loved for a while and forgotten.

These simply phrased sentences—on the next-to-last page of the book—should be placed beside the next-to-last page of *Remembrance of Things Past*:

For after death, time withdraws from the body, and the memories—so pale and insignificant—are effaced from her who no longer exists, and soon will be from him whom they still torture, and the memories themselves will perish in the end when the desire of a living body is no longer there to keep them alive.

The annihilation of memory, a theme of modern literature that has terrified and gripped the imagination of writers from Proust to Eliot and Hemingway, is Wilder's ultimate fear. He overcomes it with the bridge at the end—and has already done more than that in presenting the permanence of the Marquesa's writing and Pio's vision of excellence. Proust overcomes it by promising a great work if time permits. *The Bridge of San Luis Rey* and Proust's last volume both appeared in 1927: without overstating the affinities, one can at least see that Wilder telescoped themes of cruelty, blindness, artistic compensation, and time, which the greater master developed in over two thousand pages.

Wilder's second novel, despite some damaging passages, earns its place among the moderns. Its irony at the expense of myopia and inhumanity, its series of finely inlaid portraits, its ambitious plunge into the chaos of

chance happenings and diseased hearts, make it anything but a conventional book.

While *The Woman of Andros* is closely related in its
themes to the earlier novels, it represents a slackening of
Wilder's energies. In one sense a part of the literature of
the 1920s because of its obsessive concern with the isolated self, the book is in another sense old-fashioned because of its message-mongering and its heavy display of
sentiment. The reader encountering the book after *The
Cabala* and *The Bridge of San Luis Rey* suspects that
Wilder has become so comfortable with his themes of
damaged lives and isolation that he took to stating them
directly rather than exerting himself to embody them in
a complex structure.[7] Once noticed, however, this falling off should not cancel out the novel's merits, which
are its often distinguished prose style and its intellectual
ambitions.

The plot structure is different from that of the first
two novels. While the earlier books were held together
by portrait sections that caught the drama of individual
lives, *The Woman of Andros* is a conventional linear
story, freely adapted from Terence's *Andria,* which is
untouched by the earlier bizarre twists and eruptions of
chance and human emotions. The plot deals with an Al-
exandrine courtesan who has come to the Greek island of
Brynos some time in the century before Christ. Chrysis,
a cultured and deeply sensitive woman, has established
herself as mentor and symposium leader for the local
young men. Wilder refines the woman's profession out
of existence as he paints her in the almost saintly colors
of a Socrates, a reflector on the mysteries of the human
situation. Each evening her young men foregather to
discuss such questions as war and peace, the fate of
women, and the meaning of suffering. One of their number, a highly gifted youth named Pamphilus, has impressed her with his depth of feeling and his superiority
to his less mature friends. Chrysis' growing love for

Pamphilus—and the obstacles in the path of such feeling—create the first conflict of the book. Pamphilus is
the son of Simo, a substantial citizen who has lived his
life entirely within the boundaries of Greek customs and
tradition; Simo's son, a taster of new ideas and fre-
quenter of a disreputable house, is a source of anxiety for
this good-hearted but narrow-minded patriarch. The father and his very simple wife—an anachronistic figure
who seems more at home in Westchester than in ancient
Greece—wants the young man to marry Philomena, a
conventional village girl. While Pamphilus—true to the
pattern of Wilder's early representations of love relationships—does not return Chrysis' affections, he nevertheless has moved far beyond his parents' purview. He falls
in love with Glycerium, Chrysis' younger sister; this shy
girl has been hidden away by her guardian sister, but, after meeting Pamphilus, she yearns for the real world of
involvement.

The book's second conflict involves what happens
when Glycerium says that she is pregnant by Pamphilus.
Chrysis, who throughout the narrative has suffered because of her undeclared passion, soon confronts the next
phase of life's tragic cycle: she is dying of cancer just as
the young lovers' affections are struggling to develop.
Not the first of Wilder's women sages, she is a spiritual
kin of the Marquesa and of Emily in *Our Town:* en-
dowed with insight into the depth of pain, she is also
marked by an ability to see into humanity's limitations.
The redeeming complexity in her nature—and, indeed,
in the book itself—is that the dark side of human affairs
is no more real than the light: the intertwining of pain
and pleasure, tragic degeneration and joyous experience, makes life into an ungraspable, endlessly ironic series of revelations.

Chrysis dies and leaves her legacy: "Remember me
as one who loved all things and accepted from the gods
all things, the bright and the dark." Glycerium, almost

sold into slavery when her sister's household is broken up, is saved by Simo but dies in childbirth. In the final recognition of Pamphilus, Wilder brings us back to the spirit of the last page of *The Bridge of San Luis Rey* as Pamphilus "too praised the whole texture of life, for he saw how strangely life's richest gift flowered from frustration and cruelty and separation."

With such a resolution, Wilder was bound to fall afoul of the critics: out of step with the cynicism of Hemingway, another writer who treated the disaster of modern love in *A Farewell to Arms,* Wilder seems to have rejected the tendency of his age. After the death of Catherine, Hemingway's Frederic Henry turns away from the texture of his life, declaring that destruction and dissolution characterize the universe:

If people bring so much courage to this world the world has to kill them to break them, so of course it kills them. The world breaks every one and afterward many are strong at the broken places. But those that will not break it kills. It kills the very good and the very gentle and the very brave impartially. If you are none of them you can be sure it will kill you too but there will be no special hurry.

This passage—a famous example of Hemingway's 1920s philosophizing—distills the attitude of the Lost Generation. In *The Woman of Andros,* Wilder seems to present an oblique answer to the affront that Hemingway offered to the ideas of progress and purpose. An anxious author grappling with the challenge of postwar disillusionment, Wilder confronts Hemingway's chaos and anguish not by simply rejecting them (the mark of the old-fashioned sentimentalist), but by using their very terms in the suffering of his people. Nearly every page of Wilder's flawed novel is marked by his genuine sense of modern disaster. Wilder's adaptation of Terence, it should be noted, destroys the happy ending of the Roman dramatist's domestic play and substitutes his own story of pain and irreparable loss. Even though Wilder loses his balance in the end by suggesting that the ancient world's suffering would take on meaning with the coming of Christ, he still manages to leave us with a sense of mystery about our universe of chance. Yet once this is granted, his didacticism does not dissolve. The book is damaged by the narrator's tedious sermonizing about the Christian future.

Perhaps even more serious is what Edmund Wilson has called Wilder's "mawkish" effects.[8] In *The Woman of Andros,* the strangeness of *The Cabala* and *The Bridge* give way to two tearful stories—complete with Chrysis moaning aloud and Glycerium trying to jump into her sister's grave. While *The Bridge* is a kind or moral conundrum, this novel often seems like "a broken-hearted Proustian sob which has welled up, all too unmistakably from the peculiar sentimentality of our own time and not from any state of mind that one can associate with the Greeks."[9] But the problem can be narrowed down further: Wilder has transferred the emotional capital of his previous two novels to a set of characters who are incapable of bearing such weight; without the bite and wit of the Marquesa or the genuine hysteria of Alix, these exhausted lovers lapse into speechmaking and declarations of feeling. It is difficult to feel the impact of their selfhoods—or cite interesting flaws in character that make them memorable. They dissolve into a theme.[10] Mike Gold's famous invective—a piece that calls the book "a synthesis of all the chambermaid literature, Sunday school tracts, and boulevard piety there ever were"—makes the moralizing seem more obtrusive than it actually is. It also completely ignores the frail characterization while it uses all its steam to denounce Wilder's attitude.

Despite his righteousness and thin character rendering Wilder did achieve two things in the novel: the adaptation of Greek ideas in a modern narrative, and the preservation of his special philosophical style. In the spirit of Plato's *Phaedrus*—a work quoted at length within Wilder's text—Wilder set out to discourse on the nature and mystery of love. Like the *Phaedrus, The Woman of Andros* has a bearer of truth and light, Chrysis; a central conflict about the seeming impossibility of a fulfilled earthly love; a resolution involving reverence for human erotic impulses; and a series of social forces and opinions that suppress the instincts. Chrysis' opponents—whether parents who understand only the legal dignity of marriage or young men who hold women up to ridicule—are Wilder's twentieth-century attempts to continue the form of dialectic of Plato. Certainly Wilder is not the most talented modern author to adapt Greek thought into fiction: from Pater to Joyce and beyond, British letters have derived substance from the ancients' attempts to puzzle out the nature of emotions. But Wilder is the most conspicuous American writer of his generation when it comes to integrating the very modern theme of isolation with the age-old question of love's nature and value. Wilder's relationship to literary modernism—and here some of our best critics would laugh or raise their eyebrows—is extremely complex and apparent even in a weak book like *The Woman of Andros*. His brother Amos Wilder tried to explain the attraction/ recoil that Thornton had for the spirit of the age of Joyce and Eliot. A consistent defender of modernist achievements, Thornton nevertheless questioned what Amos calls the "dogmas" of the age—iconoclasm and relentlessly cultivated alienation. Searching for deeper continuities with past literature and looking to integrate the modern and classical outlooks in his own work, Wilder succeeds in being an ambitious writer whose works are amalgamations of attitudes and elements. Such fusions do not always make for clarity—and do not invite praise for boldness of statement and intention.

Half twentieth-century man in his grim recogni-

tions about the limitations and desperations of human
existence, half ancient Greek in his search for transcendence, Wilder is a novelist who suffers from the complexity of his identity. On the one hand, Pamphilus uses
language that registers a recognition of modern anguish
and nihilism; the young man looks at his parents:

It seemed suddenly as though he saw behind the contentment
of the daily talkativeness into the life of their hearts—empty,
resigned, pathetic and enduring. It was Chrysis' reiterated
theory of life that all human beings—save a few mysterious ex-
ceptions who seemed to be in possession of some secret from
the gods—merely endured the slow misery of existence, hid-
ing as best they could their consternation that life had no wonderful surprises after all and that its most difficult burden was
the incommunicability of love.

This is the twentieth-century part of Wilder's identity
—located not far from Hemingway's view of the old man
in "A Clean, Well Lighted Place"; it sees emptiness and
a pathetic round of suffering. While it is, as we have in-
dicated, not the major chord in the novel, it is nevertheless struck: critics who see only the sentimentality have
not read the book with care.

But struggling against this point of view is another
Wilder. The other side of this dialogue about whether
human love can give meaning to life adapts Socrates'
point of view and puts it into the mouths of the same
characters who use a twentieth-century attitude to express their existential torment. The linchpin of Platonic
thought—that the human mind can move from its own
pettiness to a perception of reality—is what Wilder uses
as his affirmation. The main characters in the book—
Pamphilus, Chrysis, the father, Simo—move into the
light of understanding and compassion as they move
away from the shadows of their own disillusionment,
prejudice, and parochialism. Simo's words sum up the
Platonic search for transcendence—and the doubt that

we must live in most of the time: "And I am still asking myself which is the real life: the present with its discontent, or the retrospect with its emotion?" This pursuit of the "real life" gives magnitude to Wilder's book, although it is unable to compensate the reader for the deficiencies of character realization. Wilder works out the theme more satisfactorily in later books—and fuses the natures of his people with their spiritual ambitions. For now, he has only an idea without live people to carry it across his plot.

The style of the novel is another indication of Wilder's very considerable ambitions. From *The Cabala* and *The Bridge* onward, Wilder had been perfecting several stylistic strategies: the bristling ironic epigram, the inlaid character portrait, the use of the pathetic fallacy, and the echoing of masters. The first two ploys are not to be found in *The Woman of Andros*, and the book suffers from their absence. But the opening page of the novel, like *The Cabala*, is charged by the pathetic fallacy. Compare the first sentence, "The earth sighed as it turned in its course" with the opening of *The Cabala*:

It was Virgil's country and there was a wind that seemed to rise from the fields and descend upon us in a long Virgilian sigh, for the land that has inspired sentiment in the poet ultimately receives its sentiment from him.

Four years later, Wilder was sounding the same chord. Both books also end with stars carrying a sense of wearied affirmation: "The shimmering ghost faded before the stars" and "In the East the stars shone tranquilly down upon the land that was soon to be called Holy." Looked at unsympathetically, the stylistic repetition might suggest that Wilder is beginning to parody himself in *The Woman of Andros*. But the shape of Wilder's development as an artist suggests that the pathetic fallacy is no mere lapse into convenient rhetoric or purple scene painting. The plays of the late 1920s and 1930s—and the novels that come later—are relentlessly concerned with man's conviction that the earth, heavens, and sea are saying something to him and that his existence transcends the petty routine of personal affairs. Although his style—often studded with sentences like "A confused starlight, already apprehensive of the still unrisen moon, fell upon the tiers of the small houses"—is philosophical, *The Woman of Andros* has not, and surely will not earn the respect accorded to works of Hemingway and Faulkner that explore man's destiny and relationship to the cosmos. Yet the novel deserves to be seen as a quiet attempt to join his greater contemporaries in their investigation of order and chaos, belief and despair: its place, somewhere between the modern world of dread and the classic world of transcendence, makes it as uneasy and anxious a work as those of other moderns; its style is a plain, clear, and subtle vehicle that takes its images from the permanent collection of man's universe and that will later be employed to handle more convincing people and more strongly conceived themes.

3

Strange Discipline: Wilder's One-Act Experiments

Wilder's one-act plays are short journeys packaged in modern experimental forms, highly charged minutes in which he arranges his obsesessions into new arresting patterns. During the 1920s and early 1930s—and again in the late 1950s—he turned to small structures in order to concentrate his meaning. No "idea was too grandiose . . . for me to try and invest it in this strange discipline." His themes are no different from those of the early novelistic period: the awesome and strange feelings generated by being alive in a world larger than ourselves, the isolation of existence, the possibility that love is redemptive and not destructive, the irony and ridiculousness of human plans and desires. But for all the continuity, there is a radical change in shape; the plays draw attention to their form, whereas the novels—for all Wilder's affinities to the modernist tradition—are generally quieter in their effects. The one-act plays—whether those in *The Angel That Troubled the Waters* (1928), or *The Long Christmas Dinner and Other Plays in One Act* (1931)—are crafted in ways that upset conventional theater expectations and that create new recognitions.

Dispensing with well-made plots, illusions of real events taking place on stage, conventions of the box stage with actors looking out at an audience, and people whose destinies proceed from previously established patterns of action, Wilder in effect breaks with the nine-teenth-century theater of realism. While he is subtle rather than bold in his assault on the trappings of the well-made play, he is nevertheless a writer whose best short dramas are likely to become classics of American stage innovation. Often he selects unpromisingly ordi-nary or familiar material: the rituals of Christmas dinner, bedtime on a train, a car ride across a state. He likes to dramatize what playwrights generally leave out or sum up in a line. His subject matter and settings are given in-tensity and power because he seems, as Edmund Wilson has said of Sherwood Anderson, to have discovered per-manent truths all by himself—and for the first time. This freshness of approach—at first a mystery to a thea-tergoer who wonders why his attention is captured by characters who say good-bye to each other on a street in Newark—is actually the result of technical experiments and subtle dislocations.

Wilder's one-act works typically do not experiment with dialogue and diction. Their assault on the conven-tional goes to the very heart of drama: the strategy is to attack the vital organs of a well-constructed play—plot, motivated characters, resolutions. He transplants com-ponents of his own—stage managers who interrupt the plot flow, props that draw attention to themselves, inani-mate objects that speak, visual jokes, spectacular, im-possible stage effects, undramatic repetitions. As read-ers or audience, we sometimes feel that the playwright is the strangest phenomenon in American-theater history: a man whose works are combinations of eighth-grade as-sembly plays and dramas by Strindberg or Pirandello. At once naive and capable of the most complex symbolic art, Wilder takes his place beside the other twentieth-century artists who abandon slick craftsmanship and re-place it with new and seemingly cruder techniques. Such experiments, of course, are always forays into the unknown and possibly the unsuccessful.

The Angel That Troubled the Waters is the first phase of the one-act experimentation: the plays gathered in this volume are largely closet dramas "stimulated by literature," as Gilbert Harrison has noted.[1] They are Wilder's first attempts to reject naturalistic theater, and are often engaging intellectually, if not entirely satisfying as drama. Dissolving stage logic and verisimilitude, they succeed in becoming theater pieces of the mind—strange explorations of people who labor under various kinds of stresses and obsessions. They have points of tension rather than paraphrasable plots. Sometimes preposterous and often diffuse, they are always disengaged from the traceable causalities of well-made plays. To ask if most of them would "play" is about as sensible as asking if a biblical parable would make a good movie: they are small dramas that resonate with moral implications and that play best on the stage of one's own imagination. They also dislocate the whole set of nineteenth-century-theater expectations by emphasizing extravagant or childlike, naive special effects.

Beginning with *Nascuntur Poetae*—a play about artistic initiation—Wilder embodies his themes in wild and seemingly undramatic forms. In five pages of text, the playwright makes us enter "some incomprehensible painting of Piero di Cosimo; a work of pale blues and greens." A boy in the painting has been told, by a woman in a chlamys, of the chosen—artists who now "sit apart, choosing their successors." He is to be one of their number—and the play's only conflict is his fears about the impending mission. Such a situation sounds like the effort of a prep-school student who is cultured and sensitive; yet the real charm and significance of the play are not to be found in conflict or characterization, but in a few lines and an overall confidence in its vision. The child, like Pio and the Marquesa, is to assume the role of artist-sufferer and pursuer of a love more sustaining than ordinary love. "For you there shall be ever beyond the present a lost meaning and a more meaningful love."

The boy, anticipating the Marquesa, is "not yet brave," not ready for his spiritual destiny. Wilder is fond of Dantesque imagery—"shadow of the wood," "the profound shade"; he also has set up one of his enduring themes —the isolated and anxious progress of a special soul. Protestant in its emphasis on the boy's election, clumsily Catholic in its medievalism, the play is another Wilder combination of resources.

Another apprentice work that Wilder chose to publish in 1928 is *Childe Roland to the Dark Tower Came*. Once again, there are continuities with major themes and patterns—as well as very obvious dislocations from realistic technique. The disengagements are most pronounced in the medieval setting: "The sun has set over the great marsh, leaving a yellow-brown Flemish light upon the scene." Childe Roland—the strange questor mentioned in *King Lear*, and given life by Robert Browning in his poem of agony and doubt—seeks refuge in Wilder's playlet. Wounded and seeking the peace of death after his harrowing campaign, Roland is another Wilder creation who has reached the limits of his own endurance. In the midst of Roland's pleas for admittance to the dark tower, Wilder injects a scene note that is completely out of keeping with the play's tedious, stagey dialogue: "The marsh is a little put out by all this strong feeling." Ironic and wonderfully disruptive, this touch anticipates a whole world of inappropriate, irrational effects. It is doubt and playfulness tweaking the world of serious designs.

Wilder's love of disruption and unconventional effects reaches a high point in three of the 1928 volume's most ambitious plays, *The Angel That Troubled the Waters, Hast Thou Considered My Servant Job?* and *The Flight into Egypt*. Here, Wilder has attempted religious drama on a grand thematic scale—in scripts that are no longer than half a dozen pages apiece.

The plays were written about a year and a half be-

fore publication—and so represent *The Bridge* period.
Although their quality varies considerably as they stage
conflicts about faith, human pain, and the ironic aspects
of existence, each play is outlandish and thoroughly out
of step with literary naturalism. Wilder set himself the
task, described in the foreword to the volume, of writing
a kind of religious drama that deals with "human beings
pushed to such an extreme that it resembles love." He
felt a curiosity, "the French sense of a tireless awareness
of thought," about the kinds of people whom he dealt
with in the novels, people who came to an awareness of
themselves and for whom words like "faith" and "hope"
can have real significance. Ashamed of the language of
Christian belief—words like "charity," Wilder tells us,
have been ground down by didacticism—Wilder, almost like Hemingway, has to move away from the emptiness of these words and find some new way of discovering their meaning.

His manner of doing this in *The Angel That Troubled the Waters* is so overblown, stylized, and monumen-
tal that it seems more like a baroque painting come to
life than a one-act play. A group of invalids is sitting beside the biblical pool at Bathesda awaiting the angel who
will stir the waters and give them their cure. The ostensible conflict is between a newcomer who is not severely
afflicted and another suffering man whose intense pain
has caused him to throw himself into the pool before the
angel has troubled the waters. The newcomer literally
quotes the Marquesa's line in *The Bridge*—"Let me begin again." Troubled by "this fault that bears me down,"
he seems like another version of the Marquesa. The angel reminds him of a truth that has also been developed
in *The Bridge:* "Without your wound where would your
power be?" Only a "human being broken on the wheel of
living" can understand and "serve" love. The newcomer,
like Pio or the Marquesa or Esteban, must endure until
his moment. Now if all this strikes the reader as stilted

and sentimental, he should consider Wilder's ambitions.
By no means a masterpiece, the little play nevertheless
strives to carry forward one of the conceptions of a novel
into a dramatic form; the play's almost preposterous use
of space—"A vast gray hall with a hole in the ceiling
open to the sky"—is an early attempt to bring the large-
ness of *The Bridge* and the backdrop of the Andes into
the theater world. Wilder will succeed when he aban-
dons such grandiose sets for something homelier; meanwhile, this is the beginning of an escape from the box
stage.

   Hast Thou Considered My Servant Job? is another
not altogether successful attempt to break out of naturalistic form and verisimilitude. The piece is of interest because it reverses our expectations and also mixes trickery
and spectacle with morality. Christ, not Satan, has been
"going to and fro in the earth" in this spin-off on the Book
of Job. Reversing the biblical Satan, he taunts the forces
of evil by saying that Judas would not serve unless he
was rewarded by Satan. Satan responds by handing Judas over for thirty-three years—in this time the servant
of Satan has of course betrayed Christ, but he has also
despaired of the powers of evil and hanged himself. As
Satan is about to exult in the betrayal, "Suddenly the
thirty pieces of silver are cast upward from the revolted
hand of Judas." Judas, with "the black stains about his
throat and the rope of suicide," curses Satan. Playing
in almost every line with the biblical subtext, Wilder
makes his piece into an attack on the smugness of modern pessimism and cynicism. We do not inhabit the
worst of all possible worlds, and Satan's understanding
of human nature is as simplistic as a Job's comforter or
some cheery Bible-belt preacher. Seeking a place between 1920s-style cynicism and the pieties of his father's
Puritan religion, Wilder finds it in the unpredictable
character of Judas, Christ's "beloved son" who has been
revolted by his own evil nature. That a way out of despair can be paradoxically found through despairing is of

course Wilder's highly unorthodox solution to the problem of evil. Abandoning sense and stage logic, he opts for a stunning moment of awareness; Judas becomes an emblem of the way to a higher spirituality—a kind of salvation through dread and self-loathing, not unlike that proposed by modern existentialists.[2]

The Flight into Egypt is by far the most successful and engaging of the 1928 one-act plays: in a few pages it manages to do all the things that earlier plays attempted; it also dispenses with pretentiousness, scales down effects, and adopts a contemporary idiom that is both charming and highly ironic. The protagonist is a donkey named Hepzibah, the animal who bore Christ and Mary in their flight. The plot is another of Wilder's journeys —this time a few minutes of tension with Herod's soldiers in pursuit. Hepzibah is no ordinary-talking, moralizing animal out of an exemplary tale or fable. Instead, Wilder has turned the Bible story into a collision between an extraordinary event and an ordinary creature; speaking in the tone and with the genial knowingness of a New York taxicab driver, the donkey becomes a humorous, complaining, helpful, and ever-curious example of the modern self as it encounters and tries to make sense of the world's glory and misery. During most of the flight Hepzibah is unaware of her burden: she stops to rest her legs and to emphasize a half dozen points about "the whole political situation" in Palestine. While philosophizing, the donkey touches on just about every Wilder theme we have encountered so far: this latest thinker is "at home in ideas of all sorts"—faith versus reason, fate and providence, the irony of destiny. Like Brother Juniper pondering the fates of the five victims, Hepzibah wonders about the slaughtered infants:

Even in faith we are supposed to use our reason. No one is contented to swallow hook, line and sinker, as the saying is. Now take these children that Herod is killing. Why were they born, since they must die so soon? Can any one answer that?

Such a display of old chestnuts scales down the ambitions of the play while paradoxically giving it resonance. In another context, Donald Haberman has remarked that "By eliminating clichés of staging, he [Wilder] is able to offer the clichés of life as one kind of truth."[3]

The observation applies well to Wilder's overall strategy. His stage consists of an old cyclorama from a dime museum: the Holy Land rolls by in the background as a highly stylized scene is played out before us. This abandonment of the realistic set for the conventions of the grammar-school play is Wilder's way of forcing the audience back to his language: the rudimentary set, stripped of his earlier pretenses, is a complement to the awkward, clumsy first-order questions of the average mind in its pursuit of meaning. The staging also creates an ironic contrast to the magnitude of the subject matter: abandoning the bizarre and exotic for the homely, Wilder ceases to overstate; the effect makes the little piece an unusual exploration of a religious theme. A talking donkey, clanking metal for Herod's army, the Tigris and Euphrates projected on the cyclorama, make for a small drama about the inappropriate and sometimes ridiculous nature of spiritual experience. Put in Hepzibah's terms, "It's a queer world where the survival of the Lord is dependent on donkeys."

The experiments in the 1931 plays published as *The Long Christmas Dinner and Other Plays in One Act* are a continuation and development of *The Flight into Egypt*. The three best of them are also journeys— through space and years. Thematically, Wilder seems to be offering us small occasions on which we may discover who we are.

The title play, *The Long Christmas Dinner*, lacks the charming comic touches of the small religious play about the flight, but it employs several stage techniques and a series of rising ironies to provide the audience with an even more arresting view of the strangeness of human

life. The central conceit of the play—having generations
of a family reveal their enduring concerns and sufferings
at successive Christmas dinners—is perfectly fitted to
Wilder's conception of human ambitions set against the
terrifying backdrop of time. The dining room of the Bayards is the scene in which Wilder stages a concern that
he explored in *The Cabala* and *The Bridge of San Luis
Rey:* the awesome spectacle of men and women enmeshed in petty concerns and accelerating toward
death.[4] While his proscenium stage is conventional
enough here, his reinvention of its resources is highly
imaginative. Exit from stage left "is a strange garland
trimmed with fruits and flowers": newborn children are
brought through this. The black velvet on the opposite
side of the stage indicates the door of death. Characters
appear and disappear without any lengthy preliminar-
ies—one character even takes a few steps toward the
dark side and returns, recovered from alcoholism. Wilder's people sit down each year to an invisible turkey;
they carry white wigs and shawls, which they put on to
denote age. Time passes through the use of these stage
devices and through the ironic repetitions of remarks,
clichés, and greetings of the season. Each year people
take wine for the occasion and comment on the weather,
the church sermon, and the neighbors' health. Wilder
also injects small but significant ironic changes in the
family's fortunes: as they become more prosperous, they
accumulate disease and conflict; as the house is ex-
panded, its inhabitants scatter to other places; as the
play ends, an elderly cousin, the last in the house on a
Christmas day, reads a letter about a new generation in
the East and then totters toward the dark portal.

The play is Wilder's first significant blending of
experimental technique and American subject matter.
Though universal and unprovincial in its themes, the
small drama is nevertheless situated in an American
town. The flavor and notation is midwestern, genteel,

and Protestant; the Bayards are prosperous people whose native place grows from a small settlement to a large factory town. Wilder's people are correct, conventionally religious, and self-satisfied. But the placidity and correctness of their lives is periodically punctured by Roderick's drinking, his sister's loneliness and desperation, his grandson's rudeness, and the death of a young man in World War I. The swiftly dramatized agonies of the Bayards completely destroy the substance of Mike Gold's criticisms: Wilder, rather than being this critic's tightly controlled genteel chronicler of minor miseries, is a writer involved with the inexorable facts of living; his play is about desperation, decay, the endless cycle of talk and birth and death and suffering that all must endure. No "little lavendar tragedy," the play is instead a compressed presentation of all the large forces that sweep through human lives and carry them toward the dark portal. The cleverness of its technique makes its unadorned vision bearable and the rapidity of the one-act form is perhaps the most direct way of assaulting the audience with its own fund of fleeting pleasures and permanent fears.

Pullman Car Hiawatha is a more elaborate theatrical undertaking—a play that employs the machinery and strategy of experimentalism to maximum effect. Although less emotionally resonant and terrifying than *The Long Christmas Dinner,* it too manages to direct the audience to the absurd and sometimes tragic collision between our everyday lives and our ultimate destinies. But while it is also a play about time and decay, it is, in addition, a small drama that takes a group of riders to Chicago. Less matter-of-factly dreadful than *Christmas Dinner,* it lifts the audience by offering moments of pleasure, love, optimism and casual camaraderie. We arrive at a station, not at the death portal.

The play is a series of impressions given by a diverse group of travelers and also by the scenery through which they pass; fields and towns talk—as well as people, ghosts, and dead philosophers. The plot structure is loose and takes the form of the ordinary events and sensations of an overnight train trip: looking at places along the way, getting ready for bed, dreaming, waking up, getting off. During the night a young woman dies; a madwoman raves; characters lie awake and worry or fantasize, annoy each other, or mix their trivial concerns with their deepest desires and fears. The action rises as Wilder moves us from the inhabitants of the train to the creatures of the earth, to the planets and the realm of ideas and spiritual reality. When we have reached the most abstract realm of experience, we are returned to the everyday.

The play's stage technique is a startling leap forward for Wilder. The roots of experimentalism and stage artifice are in *The Flight into Egypt,* but here the development of staging makes the play into more than a charming tryout of strategies. At least four new approaches are used to produce emotional effect: the appearance of the stage manager, the use of characters who get a chance to "think," the development of characters as actors, and the use of literary quotations as both stage jokes and devices to enrich the theme. Together these ploys make a short play into a reflexive, complex, and witty modernist work.

Wilder's stage manager directs the characters' actions and assumes acting duties himself: part director and part character, he breaks down the naturalistic connections and causes the play to unfold in a way that directs us to texture and style. Like Pirandello's stage manager in *Six Characters in Search of an Author,* this director carries out his routine tasks—telling people when to speak, when to stop, where to stand—and at times is tempted into the action of the play itself. Wilder has softened the role of manager, made him less irascible and resistant to the drama before him than Pirandello's

short-fused director: in so doing, he has created less
stage furor and more community. *Pullman Car's* manager becomes one of the first real American people/
actors who give the audience a sense that the reality of a
theater and the reality of their lives are intertwined.
In gathering diverse elements together—"the whole
solar system, please. Where's the tramp?—Where's the
moon?"—the manager becomes a negotiator of the fantasies and mundane events of our lives. The word
"please"—as well as all the cues and asides and stage
directions—directs us to the acts of theater, to the fact
that they are both conjured events and practical move-
ments. Because of the stage manager, nothing happens
in the play unless we watch the sheer physicality of its
happening.

Supporting this strategy are Wilder's more general
liberties with characters. Like Pirandello, he makes
them self-conscious actors, often unsure of what they are
doing and why. But Wilder is unlike Pirandello in *Six
Characters* in at least two respects: his actor/characters
do not lead him into subtle philosophical speculations,
and his technique for revealing theme involves more
fantasy. So it is that "Grover's Corners, Ohio" appears as
a character: the guiding stage direction—"in a foolish
voice as though he were reciting a piece at a Sunday
School entertainment"—provides for even more exaggeration and artificiality. "The Field"—with gophers,
mice, and bugs—speaks next; as the play builds to its
climax, moving out of the earthly realm into the philosophical and theological, it introduces hours as philosophers who quote Plato, Aristotle, and Epictetus—and
then the planets with their humming representing the
music of the spheres; the archangels come next. After
these we have two people, the Insane Woman and Harriet, the young wife, who tell about two of Wilder's abiding concerns: misunderstood suffering and the mistake
of not having realized one's life. The Insane Woman is

another of Wilder's hysterics—people strangely damaged by life who cry out in protest. "Use me. Give me
something to do," she says; the line directs us back to the
Marquesa in *The Bridge*. Harriet, the young wife who
dies on the train, directs us forward to *Our Town:* after
death she surveys the world, like Emily; as she looks
back, she feels "I was angry and sullen. I never realized
anything." Other characters who appear in this essentially plotless play include the archangels, Michael and
Gabriel—in blue suits, the ghost of a German railroad
worker killed in an accident, a worker in a lower berth
who quotes Kipling, and a Pullman porter who has trouble thinking out loud according to the manager's cues.
Surveying the realms of being—and keeping a steady
eye on love, death, pleasure, and human diversity
—Wilder brings his trainload to Chicago. "This train
don't go no further," the porter says.

The Wilder imprint can also be found in his constant deployment of literature: mixing folk sayings, Bart-
lett-type quotations, and philosophical passages, he allows the words of others to do part of his work. No need
to have his characters freshly discovering life's pleasure:
"What is so rare as a day in June? Then, if ever, come
perfect days." The old chestnut, quoted by "The Field,"
is dramatically a joke because of the speaker, but it still
carries meaning. Similarly, Wilder avoids the pompous
and pretentious by using "beautiful girls dressed like
Elihu Vedder's Pleiades" to deliver lines of Plato, Aristotle, and Saint Augustine. Combining theater glitter
and speculation about beauty and human passion, these
figures are the typical creation of a writer who is more
concerned with fusing realms of experience through experimentation than with any kind of plot logic. One of
the most crowded small plays in American drama, *Pullman Car* is also pleasingly heavy with its writer's
techniques.

A much simpler and perhaps greater work is *The*

Happy Journey to Trenton and Camden. This one, another American trip, reveals its themes without the complex machinery of the experimentalist's techniques. The
stage manager does no more than read the lines of minor
characters "with little attempt at characterization." The
stage experiment that disappears is replaced by a quiet,
highly concentrated and unadorned presentation of the
cycle of human pleasure and pain. As a dramatic plot,
the *Journey* does no more than carry Ma Kirby, her husband, and children from their Newark house to the
Camden house of Ma's married daughter, Beulah. Like
Pullman Car, this play uses ordinary sights, trivial
exchanges, and small occurrences to draw out large
themes. But the *Journey* is stripped bare of fantastic elements and literary allusions. Confined to the mundane
from start to finish, Wilder's people dignify the ordinary
because they discover permanent truths about their
world. Without condescending or sentimentalizing, Wilder treats a limited world and draws unlimited thematic
capital from it. A car trip becomes an occasion for cosmic
recognitions.

The play is so down-scaled in its techniques and so
overtly undramatic in its subject matter that the onlooker almost forgets how tightly packed with meaning it
is. Ma Kirby matter-of-factly delivers Wilder's themes in
lines that are as plain as paint, but somehow never flat.
Truisms and clichés are freshly polished and come out as
forgotten realizations. Ma lives by an easily articulated
code of decency, friendliness, love, and pride. She is the
picture of petty-bourgeois, ungenteel health: unlike the
characters in early plays and novels, she is unencum-
bered by the neuroses, fears, and guilts of better-bred
people. She corrects children, only to be warm and loving with them; she respects conventions, but knows her
own mind; she likes order and discipline, but knows that
life is too complex to live by strict codes. Her only non-
negotiable point is the goodness of God and the essential

goodness of man.[5] Wilder has transferred this theme, first encountered in *The Bridge,* into an American context: what was once a matter of Brother Juniper's theorizing is now a practical and abiding faith. The final recognition of the play—our understanding that daughter Beulah had a child that died at birth—is something already seen in *The Flight into Egypt* and *The Bridge*. The idea of loss and suffering is dealt with so unpretentiously that one cannot help but respect the victims: "God thought it best, dear. God thought it best. We don't understand why. We just go on, honey, doin' our business." The next moment Ma is saying, "What are we giving the men to eat tonight?" While better minds offer fuller answers to the problem of human misery, Ma Kirby endures.

With such a vision, Wilder of course leaves himself open to the charge of provinciality and sentimentality. Can a writer produce a distinguished piece of theater when his protagonist and spokeswoman is someone who declares, "I live in the best street in the world because my husband and children live there"? How can a man steeped in Joyce and Proust and the classics lapse into park-bench philosophizing? If there is no irony in the portraits of the Kirbys, how can the modern audience, with tastes developed by Beckett and Strindberg, find resonance in this play? To begin with, Wilder's journey causes his people to wonder: it is anything but narrow. Arthur, the son, realizes in a few minutes, "What a lotta people there are in the world." No more than a line, this observation sets the family against the same kind of awesome backdrop we have seen in *Pullman Car Hiawatha*. As for sloppy sentimentality, one can only note that Wilder's people are too abrupt and matter-of-fact to wallow in emotions. A feeling may be unabashedly displayed, but Wilder's strategy is usually to follow it with some very ordinary fact or observation. Ma speculates on George Washington's veracity; Arthur's next line is about

an Ohio license plate. Finally, this small play has a claim
on contemporary audiences because of its homemade
and courageous assembling of very familiar themes:
without conceding to sophistication, conventional welt-
schmerz, or any attitude of the 1930s, it succeeds in being so old-fashioned as to be almost dateless. Although it
lacks the bite and irony of Joyce handling the bourgeois
mentality, it offers its own austere vision of the way
things are for millions of people. Along with heavy
championing of home and family, it is still a play about
fears, struggles, and disasters.

During the late 1950s, Wilder conceived the ideas
for two one-act play cycles—the first to be devoted to
"the seven ages of man," the second covering "the seven
deadly sins." Returning to the impulse of his youth—
especially the tendency to envision great themes embodied in small forms—Wilder again made the mistake
of miscalculating his ability to execute, polish, and con-
clude such projects. Just as most of the three-minute
plays never emerged on paper or on a stage, the new enterprises remain for us in ruins.[6] Only two of these plays
were published in his lifetime; only three were ever produced. *Infancy* and *Childhood* had skillful New York
productions and were made available to readers; other
plays in this cycle are in bits and pieces and available at
Yale University. Of "The Seven Deadly Sins," only the
sin of lust reached final form in *Someone from Assisi;* two
other works are "completed" in the sense that they are
fully drafted. Yet, Wilder never saw fit to release them
for publication or production.

This disappointing record should not obscure the
great worth of the plays that saw the light of day. The
two "seven ages" plays carry forward early themes, but
do so in an almost uncategorizably charming, witty, and
experimental form. Writing at the time when "the theater of the absurd" was a dominant force in the work of
many important playwrights,[7] Wilder shares the spirit of

his age in his technique while dramatizing material that
is all his own. Delicacy, subtlety, rich humor, and firm
commitment to the humanist's position characterizes the
late work. While compeers with great literary ambitions,
like Beckett and Ionesco, explored the desperation of
the human situation in bizarre forms—bums in *Waiting
for Godot* waiting for nothing, men changing into rhinos
in *Rhinoceros*—Wilder charted the American family's development in a deeply ironic, optimistic, and
comic style. Building on the sly humor of *The Flight into
Egypt* and the grim irony of *The Long Christmas Dinner*, he adds several new applications of irony, word
play, and stage disjunction. In the manner of his exuber-
ant, richly textured, and complex comedy, *The Skin of
Our Teeth*, he builds comic effects: once again he uses
Joyce's stream of consciousness and dreamlike effects to
reproduce a world that we would otherwise not have ac-
cess to—that of infancy and childhood. No myopic adult
writing about childlike characters, he becomes a comic
voyager willing to immerse himself in the impressions,
fantasies, and impulses of a distant period in human development. Along with this Joycean frankness and sense
of adventure—the impulse that led Joyce to begin *A
Portrait of the Artist as a Young Man* with a child telling
about a moo cow and the sensations of infancy—Wilder
adds the stage dimension of the ridiculous; in the manner of the absurd playwrights, he uses full-grown men in
baby carriages, adults who are parodies of maturity in
their mechanical and ludicrous behavior, a whole array
of clichés and misunderstanding for dialogue. While the
plays of the 1930s were an essentially serious look at the
family's destiny, these new works are infused with the
comic-absurd spirit.

The concerns of the two later one-act plays seem to
be foreshadowed in several journal entries from 1956. At
that time Wilder was still trying to overcome the organi-
zational difficulties of his Norton lectures on the Ameri-

can character. The focus of his book was to be disconnec-
tions, especially the ways that Americans are cut off from
the social dependencies of Europeans and isolated in
their own individualism. This theme, nothing new for
the writer of *The Cabala* or *The Bridge,* was especially
applicable to Emerson, Wilder's intellectual villain in
the national letters: he argued that Emerson's spiritual
happiness was separated from the happiness and woe of
humanity. Emerson's "sufficiency"—always a pejora-
tive term for Wilder—was an irrational and dangerous
strain in American thought, an intellectual heirloom that
Wilder was attempting to discard in his own late work.
Wilder experimented with the idea of inserting transi-
tional passages in the Norton lectures about a prototypical American character, one Tom Everage—an average,
middle-class neurotic—troubled by his inability to connect his life with the world around him. A prisoner of
fears, hatreds, and haunting memories, Tom was destined for a life of frustration—and perhaps violence.
Wilder planted the seeds of his one-act cycle by refer-
ring to Tom's "infancy" as the period when the "frustrated emperor" was "crossed and obstructed at every
turn." This Freudian allegory, combined with Wilder's
own ideas of isolation, did not work in the lectures, but it
enriched and shaped *Infancy* and *Childhood*—two plays
about disconnectedness, isolation, and the situation of
the lonely self.

Infancy: A Comedy in One Act is an outlandish look
at two babies' world of frustration and isolation. A counterpointed story like *The Bridge,* it tells about the infantile struggle of Tommy and Moe while presenting the
more trivial struggles of Miss Millie Wilchick, Mrs.
Baker, and Officer Avonzino. The scene is Central Park
in the twenties, and the characters are deliberately caricatured types, reminiscent of figures from the early
screen and vaudeville. Millie is a dim-witted baby nurse
whose mind is filled with plots of dime-store romances;

Officer Avonzino is part Keystone Cop—angry and equipped with billy club—and part Chico Marx with his shrewdness and his heavy Italian accent; Mrs. Baker is a Jewish mother whose precocious baby is driving her crazy. The babies are curious, aggressive, grasping, sexually aware monsters out of Freud. Tommy listens as Miss Millie quotes from a novel: "He drew her to him, pressing his eyes on hers." The infant mouths the words and immediately declares, "Wanta make a baybee!" He absorbs every adult concern, sniffs out every smell of food, and rages because he cannot obtain the pleasure that he imagines. Moe is another "genius" in a carriage—or one of the "ingeniouses" as Officer Avonzino calls him: he is skilled at manipulating his parents, watching their every move, and exploring the realms of sex and self-assertion. His father thinks he is dirty-minded; his mother acknowledges him as a master of domination. "I don't have to tell you what life with a baby is: (Looking around circumspectly.) It's war—*one long war.*" Or as Officer Avonzino puts it, "All you babies want the whole world."

The play succeeds brilliantly in employing the comic mode for the purpose of exploring another dimension of our humanity. Often rationalized by creative writers, the world of childhood is a chaos of impulses that are not easily represented. Wilder focuses on the life force—the baby's rage to assert himself. This should be no surprise to the audiences familiar with Wilder's sanguine view of human potential: even the earliest plays assert the achievements of the human spirit, the drive to learn and progress. The journeys of the 1930s have now become the long stretch of the human lifespan.

The second stage is *Childhood,* the only other play in the cycle that Wilder chose to publish. This play is more substantial and highly crafted than *Infancy*—a witty plot and a strong emotional appeal are added to the

absurdist elements of the earlier work. Again, we are
dealing with fantasies, dreams, and aggressive wishes.
But this time, Wilder has shaped his play to show the
movement out of infantile self-absorption. While *Infancy* explores isolation and rage, this small drama is
about recognition of otherness; its theme is the growth of
the child into the world of comprehension and tolerance.
Three children and their parents are involved in this latest journey into knowledge: Wilder uses a game "which
is a dream" to take his characters to the next plateau of
recognition. Caroline, twelve; Dodie, ten; and Billee,
eight, go on a "bus ride" and discover what their parents
are like for the first time.

The plot line begins with the children's gruesome
and funny world of play. "Hospital" and "orphans" are
their two favorite games—the latter of course involving
the pleasures of destroying their masters. Filled with resentment, the children express their loneliness and fear:
parents go on trips to sick relatives and stay for years;
they drink and scold and understand nothing. They
never say or do anything "inneresting." They deserve to
die as a punishment for being aliens. The parents, in
turn, regard the children as strangers and interlopers.
Occupied with their own routines and impatient with
what they cannot understand, they too yearn for release.
The father has a dream about a Mediterranean cruise
where they are "somehow . . . alone." The early turning
point in the development of the action comes when the
father begins to reflect and asks "just once" to be "an invisible witness to one of my children's dreams."

From here the play takes off in a different direction—into a delightful realm of play, learning, and rec-
onciliation. The imaginary bus ride allows the three children to interact with the driver (their father) and a veiled
passenger (their mother). The main technique of this
portion is the recycling of the children's basic concerns
in the form of fantasy resolutions: whatever they have
complained about or resented is dealt with and resolved

by the bus driver. Drinking, loneliness, money problems, fear of death: each is treated with an offhanded word or two, which causes the children to move out of their world of isolated resentment into a shared existence. Of death the father says, "We don't think about that." Of drinking, he advises the eight-year-old Billee, "There'll be no liquor drinking on this bus. I hope that's understood." Of the battle to make ends meet: "Well, you know what a man's life is like, Mrs. Arizona. Fight. Struggle. Survive. Struggle. Survive. Always was." When the children decide to return home, the father's line is pure Wilder in its understated, ordinary, but emotionally charged quality—"I'll honor that ticket *at anytime,* and I'll be looking for you." Sentiment, to be sure, but the touch is so quick and deft that it never descends to sentimentality.

Wilder did not move much further with the "ages of man" project. The imaginative engine that produced non-naturalistic drama in several modes broke down in the early 1960s. Employing literature, history, and biblical motifs in the 1920s, popular American culture and the social life of ordinary people in the 1930s, Wilder finished his work in the 1960s as a one-act playwright by turning to smaller scenes and the psychic struggles of human development. From literature and art to society and self: the progress is away from the highly artificial, stylized, hothouse world of early plays about Childe Roland and Job. In the middle of his progress he reached the high point of his art: a balancing of his early aesthetic concerns against later psychological themes. The three most important plays, *Our Town, The Merchant of Yonkers,* and *The Skin of Our Teeth,* represent a harmonizing of techniques; neither isolated in old books nor limited to the self's concerns, they are social plays and plays about civilization. They continue the experimentalism of the 1930s work: but they are also much larger in scope and much deeper in their emotional reaches.

4

The Major Full-Length Plays: Visions of Survival

After seeing a production of *Our Town* in 1969, a young girl from Harlem commented to a *New York Times* reporter that she was unable to identify with the characters and situations.[1] Grover's Corners, New Hampshire, was a completely alien place and its people were in no way relevant to her concerns. Such a response is not singular or especially unsympathetic. From its first tryouts in Princeton prior to the original New York production in 1938, the play has met with significant critical and popular resistance. If it isn't the distance of the urban audience from Wilder's small-town setting and values, it is a matter of contemporary sensibility or fear of sentimentality, or unease about the play's obsession with mortality, or lack of familiarity with unconventional theatrical forms. New York audiences did not immediately take to a play with no scenery and a last act that was set in a graveyard. Mary McCarthy, writing for *Partisan Review*, was favorable in her reactions, but somewhat ashamed that she liked the play. "Could this mean that there was something the matter with me? Was I starting to sell out?"[2] Miss McCarthy's review was careful to take shots at the scene between Emily and George: "Young love was never so baldly and tritely gauche" as this. She also made sure that readers of *Partisan* knew that *Our Town* was "not a play in the accepted sense of the term. It is essentially lyric, not dramatic." With this comment she was able to set the play apart from great modern dramas of movement and characterization like *Six Characters in Search of an Author* or *Miss Julie:* she could like the play without acknowledging that it was fully a play. On an emotional level, Eleanor Roosevelt also responded ambivalently—"Yes, *Our Town* was original and interesting. No, it was not an enjoyable evening in the theatre."[3] She was "moved" and "depressed" beyond words. Edmund Wilson's reaction was similarly complicated: Wilder remarks in a letter that Wilson was "so moved that you found yourself trying to make out a case against it ever since" (January 31, 1938). Wilson's later pronouncement (letter to Wilder, June 20, 1940) that *Our Town* was "certainly one of the few first-rate American plays" is far less revealing about his emotional reaction than the earlier response. Wilder's play, in short, had its difficulties with general Broadway audiences, with intellectuals, and with prominent people of taste and moral sensitivity. For every Brooks Atkinson who enthusiastically found "a profound, strange, unworldly significance"[4] in the play, there was an uncomfortable Mary McCarthy.

The barriers that stand between us and *Our Town* are even more formidable than those of 1938. McCarthy of course was writing as a literary modern in sympathy with the anti-Stalinist left: the commitment to experiment of the *Partisan Review* might have drawn her toward the lyric innovation of Wilder's work, but behind her reaction was an uneasiness with Wilder's sentimental situations. Other progressives of 1938, perhaps even Mrs. Roosevelt, were struck by Wilder's essentially tragic view of human potential: despite what we aspire to, we are always unaware of life around us and of the value of our most simple moments. We must face death in order to see. Such an informing theme could only cause the liberal, progressive mind to recoil. After more than forty years, audiences have accumulated attitudes,

convictions, tastes, and experiences that set them farther apart than ever. Distrust of WASP America's values, the sexual revolution, feminism, fear of America's
complacency, the resistance of many Americans to marriage and family life, the distrust of group mentalities,
the rise of ethnic literatures, the general loosening of re-
straints on language and conduct: such obstacles have
wedged their way between us and Wilder's drama. As a
scene unfolds—for example, Mrs. Gibbs being gently
chastised by her husband for staying out so late at choir
practice—the way we live now occupies the stage beside the players, mocking them and pointing up their
limitations as fully developed men and women in the
modern world.

Many of the roads that lead us to the drama of mid-
century seem to be in better shape than the Wilder road:
O'Neill and Williams deal with obsession, sexual passion, illness, and torment. Miller deals with broken
American dreams. But Wilder employs the notations of
an essentially stable and happy society. To reach his
work, we must pay more attention to the situations and
themes that he created for people such as ourselves: *Our
Town* has our themes, our fears, our confusion; Wilder
built the play so that every scene has something to reach
us. Our problem has been that whereas other American
playwrights have offered encounters with desolation and
the tragic isolation of tormented people—the themes of
the great modernists and indeed of Wilder himself in his
first two novels—Wilder's 1938 play is about another
area of our struggle: the essentially ordinary, uncomplicated, yet terrifying battle to realize fully our own ordinary existences. Such a subject obviously is more difficult to present than the more visceral situations that
many great contemporary writers have dealt with; but
Wilder's style and form are what force the concerns of
the play to become familiar truths charged with new vision.

His style and the design in the play produce the effects of American folk art: in setting, dialogue, and structure, the play comes before the audience like a late nineteenth-century painting depicting the customs, colors, and destinies of ordinary lives. Whereas O'Neill and Williams give resonance to their characters by exploring hidden motivations and desires, Wilder directs us to the bright surface and the overall pattern of his people's existences. Essentially plotless, the three acts are rooted in theme rather than dramatic movement. We do not so much wait for events or develop curiosity about characters; instead we are made to stand away from the tableau and contemplate three large aspects of earthly existence: daily life, love and marriage, death. As many folk artists do, Wilder positions us at some distance from his subjects: the audience even needs a stage manager to take us into the town and back to 1901. Like the folk artist, Wilder does not care much about verisimilitude, accurate perspective in drawing characters, and shading: "reality" does not require subtlety or many-layered characters or ingenuity of plot. Quoting Molière, Wilder said that for the theater all he needed "was a platform and a passion or two."[5]

This attitude toward his art can best be understood if we look at Wilder's plot ingredients and observe their affinities to folk art.[6] Act I is packed with natural scenery, social usages, material things, and typical encounters. The sky lightens and the "morning star gets wonderful bright." The town is presented building by building, and then the Gibbses and Webbs are shown in the foreground. Like figures in a typical folk painting, however, the two families are not drawn with careful perspective, and they are no more or no less important than the life that surrounds them in Grover's Corners. They are in the midst of the town and the universe, absorbing and emblemizing social and cosmic concerns. The stage manager dismisses people with, "Thank you,

ladies. Thank you very much" just as the folk painter
avoids focusing: Wilder's manager switches our attention
from Mrs. Gibbs and Mrs. Webb to Professor Willard
and his discourse on the natural history of the town.
Soon social life and politics are surveyed; the act closes
with a cosmic framing of the material. Jane Crofut, Rebecca Webb's friend, received a letter from her minis-
ter: after the address the envelope reads—"The United
States of America; Continent of North America; Western
Hemisphere; The Earth; The Solar System; The Universe; The Mind of God." Rebecca marvels that the post-
man "brought it just the same." This closing line—with
its reminder that the most ordinary address in an average town has a clear relationship to the cosmic order—is
Wilder's way of practicing the folk-painter's craft: Grover's Corners lies flat before us, open to the hills and fir-
mament. Every person, object, feeling, and idea takes
its place in the tableau of existence. If Wilder had taken
the route of probing Mr. Webb's psyche, he would have
ruined the simple design of his composition. Act I, in its
multifariousness and plenitude, stands as a kind of cele-
bratory offering to the universe, a playwright's highly
colored, two-dimensional rendering of living.

Act II is called "Love and Marriage" and takes place
in 1904. Once again, it does not appeal to our desire for
complex shading and perspective. Character motivation
is very simply presented: Emily has always liked
George, then has her doubts about him because he is
self-centered, and finally feels his capacity for remorse
and development. George's motivation for redirecting
his life and staying in Grover's Corners after high school
is equally direct and simple: "I think that once you've
found a person that you're very fond of . . . I mean a person who's fond of you, too, and likes you enough to be
interested in your character . . . well, I think that's just
as important as college is, and even more so." This is all
that Wilder uses to set the act in motion: no ambiva-

lence, no social complications, no disturbances. The pri-
mary colors of human love, however, do not preclude
the black terror that seizes George before his wedding.
He cries out against the pressures and publicness of getting married. Emily's response to the wedding day is no
less plaintive; why, she wonders, can't she remain as she
is? This apparently awkward doubling of fears and sor-
rows is the kind of strategy that has made Wilder seem
hopelessly out of touch with modern men and women.
Indeed, if we are looking for what Yeats called "the fury
and mire of human veins" we have come to the wrong
playwright; it is not that Wilder's lovers have no passion.
It is simply that their creator has risen above their individuality and sought to measure them against time and
the universe. What counts in the historical and cosmic
sense is that they are two more accepters of a destiny
that connects them with most of humanity: "M . . .
marries N . . . millions of them," the stage manager comments at the end of the act. Hardly a romantic, Wilder
directs us to the complete unadorned design of the human sequence. "The cottage, the go-cart, the Sunday-
afternoon drives in the Ford, the first rheumatism, the
grandchildren, the second rheumatism, the deathbed,
the reading of the will." There is no mist of feeling, no
religious sentiment, no attempt to assign high significance to the procession of events: if audiences find Act II
touching—and if some people are moved to tears—the
cause is certainly not in any overwriting and pleading
for response. Wilder's language is almost bone dry.
The stage manager's comments set the mood. As a man
who has married two hundred couples, he still has his
doubts about one of Grover's Corners' most cherished
institutions.

Act III is about death and has the form of a memo-
rial folk painting: like many pictures from the nineteenth
century that memorialized famous or obscure men and
women, Wilder's act brings in scenes from a life—in this

case Emily's is featured—and surrounds the central figure with the routines and rituals of ordinary, rather than
extraordinary, existence. A typical "important" memo-
rial piece—for instance, the death of George Washington—is filled with references to valor and public deeds;
a more modest person's life has the notation of his simple
good works. Emily's death, and by extension the deaths
of Mrs. Gibbs and lesser characters, is placed in the context of the quotidian. Newly arrived in the graveyard on
the hill, the young woman at first refuses to accept her
fate and yearns to reexperience the texture of her life.
Any day will do; but once she returns to earth on her
twelfth birthday, the details of existence—people's
voices, a parent's youthful appearance, food and coffee, the gift of a postcard album—are overpowering.
Through a clever ironic twist that both prevents the
scene from being conventionally sentimental and also
forces insight on the audience, Wilder has Emily refusing to mourn or regret. Instead, she throws the burden
of loss and blindness on the audience, on the living people who never "realize life while they live it." This very
short scene is both birthday and funeral—actually
a grim, hard look at the spectacle of human beings,
adorned by Wilder with folk motifs: habitual comings
and goings, Howie Newsome, the paperboy on his
route, breakfast being served. These details have had
the curious effect of making some audiences find *Our
Town* a cozy vision of New Hampshire life. Looked at in
relationship to their structural function—the building
up of a dense, ordinary, casual, and unfelt reality to
stand against the cosmic order—they are chilling. Like
Ivan Ilyich's curtain-hanging (which brings on his fatal
illness) or his tickets for the Sarah Bernhardt tragedy
(which he can't attend because he is dying), the Wilder
folk objects and motifs are frightening fixtures of our
lives that once gave pleasure but can only stand in Act
III for all the blindness of human existence. After having

presented us with this striking fusion of folk art and existential dread, Wilder regrettably mars the last scene
with hokum about stars and human aspirations. While
this does complete the pattern in Act I where the "Wonderful bright morning star" opens the first scene, it also
insists on a kind of message that the experience of the
play does not support: only the earth, among the planets
and stars, "is straining away, straining away all the time
to make something of itself."

This kind of didacticism is disconsonant with and
unworthy of Wilder's most fully realized scenes. The fact
is that Grover's Corners hardly strains for anything: it
isn't very progressive or cultured or enlightened or interesting. Culturally, there is *Robinson Crusoe*, the Bible, Handel's *Largo*, and Whistler's Mother—"those are
just about as far as we go." Mrs. Gibbs has cooked thou-
sands of meals. George aspires no higher than—perhaps
not as high as—his father. "Straining" to be civilized and
to make oneself into something is singularly absent from
the play's action. Wilder has instead built up something
far less sententious in his three acts: rather than give us
yet another American story of social aspiration and the
love of democratic vistas, he has used American ordinariness to embody the ardors and terrors of human existence. Tolstoy said of his existential protagonist Ivan
Ilyich, "Ivan's life was most simple and most ordinary
and therefore most terrible." Wilder would only add
"wonderful" in summing up his own characters' lives.

Wilder had a very definite sense that his play was
being manhandled by its first director, Jed Harris: the
flavoring and style of Wilder's brand of folk art were in
danger of being reduced to the level of calendar art.
Harris insisted that the language of certain scenes be
simplified—that poetry be sacrificed in the interests of
movement and stagecraft. Later on, other changes in the
play—having children cutely corrected by ever-scold-
ing, kindly parents—made the production look like the

worst kind of ersatz Americana. Wilder was infuriated that his cosmic drama was being brought down to the level of Norman Rockwell's small-town scene painting. Never a provincial, he was disturbed to find that his artful use of folk motifs could be translated into such vulgar stage forms. The folk-art techniques that he worked with were actually quite different from the flood of pictures and stories produced by local-color artists offering Americans souvenirs of New England. Wilder, of course, was not a "genuine primitive" artist: an accomplished adapter of Proustian motifs in *The Cabala* and *The Bridge*, he couldn't ever hope to have the innocence of the natural storyteller. At the same time he was not the meretricious sort of artist who fed off folk motifs and invested nothing in them. *Our Town* is one of many modern works of literature that employ abstraction, flattening, and distortion: its technique is like that of Hemingway's careful building up of a design from very simple physical details; the emphasis is on reverence for objects in themselves and the sensations that come from perceiving them. Attention to startling aspects of surface—just as Hemingway or Woolf or Picasso attend to physicality—makes *Our Town* a modernist exploration of being rather than a tendentious old-fashioned work that seeks to explain away the mystery of human and nonhuman reality through analysis. Wilder's people in *Our Town* are rarely allowed to move out of their mysterious innocence and become hokey figures who are too sophisticated for their setting and the terms of their dramatic existence. Emily—the young girl who poses the greatest threat to the play by her speechmaking about blindness and the fact that we never "look at one another"—is not allowed to spoil the play. After Emily bursts into lines about what has happened to them as a family—her brother Wally's death, the changes in fourteen years, the fact that her mother is a grandmother—Mrs. Webb answers with the reality of the

twelfth birthday on her mind. In the haunting style of
The Long Christmas Dinner, Wilder makes Mrs. Webb
offer the young girl an unnamed present in a yellow paper, "something" from the attic and the family past. The
immediacy of life—how we experience it at the time,
not how we muse about it—is Wilder's concern. The
New Hampshire details are accessible bits of the palpa-
ble world that Wilder shapes into a cosmic design: he
has little interest in them as quaint reminders of a lost
world.

Most of his play was written in a small village in
Switzerland, once again reminding us that he is the international artist like Joyce or Hemingway who stands at
a distance from his subject, respects its patterns, carefully builds its particulars, but has little interest in creating a New England period piece. The irony, of course, is
that a work with great generalizing powers can also be
received as a portrait of a specific time and place. Wilder
profited in the short run from this irony as audiences began to feel comfortable with the play that was suppos-
edly about small-town American life. But after almost
fifty years, the "American" localism is eroding his stature
among his contemporaries.

If *Our Town* is to remain alive as an American
drama, it must come before us as a play about sensations—about how we receive the concrete news of cold,
heat, food, love, joy, and death. In a letter to Edmund
Wilson, dated January 31, 1938, Wilder remarked that
his play—with its "columns of perspective on the trivial-
ities of Daily Life"—"must be some atavistic dynamite."
Since the impact of the play is not obscured by the social
problems that muddy many of O'Neill's or Miller's plays
or the sexual concerns that are likely to make Williams
inaccessible to audiences attuned to a different image of
women, Wilder is likely to stand out as an artist with a
timeless concern for "Mama's sunflowers. And food and
coffee. And new ironed dresses and hot baths . . . and

sleeping and waking up." Whether audiences will be engaged by Wilder's existential tableau or whether they will prefer fascinating new social and psychological issues is not as yet clear. But one thing is certain in the 1980s: Sam Shepard's *True West*—with its wild parody and disjointed presentation of crazed American dreams—is what occupies the minds of serious theater-goers while *Our Town* has been relegated to television and summer theater. Once said, this should not obscure the claims that the play is likely to have on future audiences. The world of the Gibbses and the Webbs is an antielitist vision of human existence that may appeal to audiences sickened by domination and brutality. Grover's Corners reminds us that affection and family loyalty animate human lives; competition and self-interest—the themes of American life in the 1980s—are overshadowed in *Our Town* by more generous recognitions. Young George's feelings of guilt come from not having helped his mother; Emily's speech about "blindness" proceeds from her own sense that willfulness and vanity have made life a painful memory. Mrs. Gibbs's small savings, which have been accumulated from the sale of an old piece of furniture, do not serve her or give Dr. Gibbs his vacation: yet unknown to Emily and George, the money gives the young couple their start in life. Wilder's interlocking world of feelings and interests is a version of life in a democratic culture to which we are so unused that it may soon become remarkable.

Only months after *Our Town* appeared on the boards in New York, Wilder offered a second full-length play. *The Merchant of Yonkers* is altogether different in style and atmosphere from the earlier work: while the world of Grover's Corners impinges on the cosmos—and uses the abstract techniques of the folk artist to universalize small-town experience—this new play is about society and employs the sparkle of the comedy of manners along with the roughhouse of farce. But for all its buoyancy, *The Merchant* deals with the darker side of human nature—capitalistic greed, exploitation, denial of vital possibilities, and neurosis. Ironically, the play that became *Hello Dolly!* is all about Horace Vandergelder, a sour Protestant businessman, and his success at manipulating those around him; Dolly Levi, the widow of a Viennese lover of life and pleasure, is Vandergelder's comic nemesis. When the Yonkers and Vienna mentalities meet, the clash becomes another one of Wilder's international studies of values. The spirit of Vienna comes to pervade this play just as the spirit of Christmas—what Louis Cazamian has called *la philosphie de Noël*[7]—suffuses many of Dickens's tales: generosity of feeling, spiritual regeneration, the affirmation of pleasure, and the adventure of life give the play the qualities of a nineteenth-century protest against grasping materialism. But the play's date, and the actions of its central character Vandergelder, should remind audiences that Wilder is working through the issues of the American Depression. This is also done as he comically explores the way the capitalistic ethos blights lives and makes the office and the home places of confinement rather than of pleasure and fulfillment.

Horace Vandergelder, a widower who has paid some attention to New York dressmaker Irene Molloy, is not merely the prototypical miser of farce. In Act I he appears as the spokesman for a point of view that had considerable currency during the 1930s: as a good, solid businessman, he preaches about the dangers of wastefulness and extravagance; apprentices and employees such as his clerks, Barnaby and Cornelius—the one an innocent of seventeen, the second a worn-down man of thirty-three—don't know the value of work and have no claim on the private sector for a better life. He believes that almost all the people in the world are spendthrifts and talkers of foolishness. Vandergelder decides to turn the nonsense of love and marriage into a practical deal—if handled correctly, a wife can be transformed into a contented drone who imagines that she has a share in a rich man's prosperity. Vandergelder embarks upon a cautious search for a wife-employee, someone to fulfill his dream of exploitation mixed with "a little risk and adventure." "Marriage," he reasons, "is a bribe to make a housekeeper think she's a householder." The crudity of this theory of relationships is a parody of the way the hard-bitten capitalist of the thirties (and indeed of the eighties) regarded those who own nothing but their labor. Wives and employees have to be made to feel part of the economy. "Did you ever watch an ant carry a burden twice its size? What excitement! What patience." In trying to work through his plans for manipulating those around him, he comes up against recalcitrant human nature: discontented workers like Barnaby and Cornelius who want to have a fling in New York; a niece who wants to marry an insolvent artist; and Dolly, a witty and charming busybody who isn't satisfied with the world as the Vandergelders have made it. Dolly, like some interfering and generous spirit, is anti-laissez-faire. "Nature is never completely satisfactory and must be corrected" is certainly a line that chills Vandergelder's sort. And money, Dolly argues, should not be "idle, frozen." "I don't like the thought of it lying in great piles, useless, motionless." Dolly believes in money as a resource for people rather than as a mechanism for asserting power. "It should be flowing down among the people, through dressmakers and restaurants and cabmen, setting up a little business here, and furnishing a good time there." Dolly too is a manipulator—and Act I ends as she talks Vandergelder into coming to New York to dine with the woman of his dreams. Dolly has it in mind to make New York a happier place—"more like Vienna and less like a collection of nervous and tired ants." Vandergelder's vision of the patient ant is comically threatened even before he goes on his ill-fated "little adventure."

Act II carries along and embroiders the themes of

exploitation and generosity, manipulation and unencum-
bered pleasure. Mrs. Molloy and her young apprentice
Minnie are trapped in their shop just as Horace and his
apprentices are trapped in their Yonkers store. Mrs.
Molloy has developed a disillusioned attitude toward
life, and intends to marry Horace for material reasons.
Like Horace, she yearns for something more—some of
the "wickedness" that milliners are supposed to enjoy.
She is ripe for the arrival of the two apprentices and for
the kindly practical joke that Dolly has in store. In the
course of the act, Cornelius and Barnaby hide from Vandergelder, accidentally provide the impression that Mrs.
Molloy is "wicked," and cause the merchant to stalk out
with Mrs. Levi. Dolly has meanwhile altered "nature"
and the reality of economics a bit by giving out the fiction that Cornelius is a bon vivant. Now that she is freed
of the practical entanglement with a man she doesn't
love, Irene Molloy is prepared for a night out—at the
expense of Cornelius, now baffled and intoxicated by a
"woman's world" and in possession of a bit more than a
dollar. But Cornelius and Barnaby have made a life-
availing pact in Act I—to have a good meal, to be in danger, to spend all their money, and not to return to Yonkers until they've kissed girls.

In Act III the complications mount as all the characters collide at the Harmonia Gardens Restaurant. Vandergelder is supposed to meet the fictitious Ernestina
Simple, a model of thrift and beauty; Cornelius and
Barnaby are treating Mrs. Molloy and Minnie; Dolly is
setting up Vandergelder for herself; the niece Ermegarde and her boyfriend are dining upstairs. In the farcical tradition, most of the relationships are temporarily
short-circuited: Vandergelder, in particular, escapes
Dolly, and the niece and the artist are still in Vandergelder's power.

Cornelius and Barnaby are fired from their positions—this time they encounter Vandergelder's wrath

when he discovers them dancing in drag. Thematically, two important points have been reached. During the evening's scuffle, Vandergelder has lost his purse—and Cornelius has had his night out at the miser's expense. Such comic disbursement—another kind of generosity—is central to the play's meaning. But Vandergelder without a purse is still not a Scrooge ready to celebrate Christmas. Dolly predicts his future: the man who is friendless, living with a housekeeper who can prepare his meals for a dollar a day. "You'll spend your last days listening at keyholes, for fear someone's cheating you." Yet even this idea of the unlived life is not enough to bring him around.

Act IV functions like a mechanical toy: it wraps up the problem and disentangles the miseries with little reference to human psychology. Vandergelder snaps out of his miserly groove and makes Cornelius his partner. Lovers are united; money is spent; greed vanishes in the dizzying atmosphere of newly found pleasure and adventure. The most believable events concern Dolly herself—once a desolate woman sitting with her Bible and hearing the bell strike at Trinity Church, she has now chosen to live among "fools" (to use Vandergelder's term) and to find some comfort and pleasure by marrying and transforming Vandergelder. Once like the dead leaf that fell from her Bible, she is now able to rejoin the human race. The privatized lives of the play—Vandergelder communing with his economic fantasies, his two employees living in innocence of life's adventure, Dolly in her room, Mrs. Molloy and Minnie shut out from pleasure, Ermegarde's aunt, Miss Van Huysen, in her lonely New York house—are propelled toward one another by an author who has now made comic capital out of his 1920s theme of the unlived life. The play's positive energy is wonderfully distilled in the line of a minor character: "Everybody's always talking about people breaking into houses, ma'am; but there are more people in the world who want to break out of houses, that's what I always say." The remark not only contains the meaning of the play's resolution; it also brings forward a theme from Wilder's early career: he has not finished his dealings with private desolation and the suffering of people enclosed by culture and neurosis. *The Skin of Our Teeth* is the next phase; *Theophilus North* the last.

For a play that has earned a reputation as a trivial farce, *The Merchant of Yonkers* offers a clever assessment of life in a competitive society. It does so, however, in the joking, slapstick manner of the commercial theater; it is also equipped, it should be added, with Freudian and Marxist insights. Bubbling out of this farcical evening is a series of observations about isolation, neurotic self-involvement, and the waste of human potential. Cornelius is a thirty-three-year-old man who has never tasted life; Dolly herself was almost the victim of isolation; Miss Van Huysen sees the young lovers' plight in the terms of her own imprisoning existence. On the socioeconomic side, Wilder employs the reasoning of Marx in *The Economic and Philosophic Manuscripts of 1844*—money is a universal solvent in bourgeois society; it dissolves and alters all human relationships.[8] A little of it, as Dolly keeps reminding us, can create a world of pleasure; the lack of it—or the Vandergelderian accumulation of it—stunts lives. Instead of presenting a cynical or bitter character, Wilder has managed to offer Dolly as a buoyant, worldly-wise woman whose major social mission is to get the juices of the capitalist system flowing. Put in Wilder's terms, the language that Dolly uses to describe money, wealth is like manure: it should be spread around to help make young things grow. Wilder has adopted the thinking of nineteenth-century writers like Dickens, Ruskin, and Marx—money is a waste product, Dickens's "dust" and Ruskin's gift of the dust, which makes society develop. Dolly's outlook, in its final form, is essentially one of compromise and accommodation to capitalist culture—like a New Deal planner, she saves Vandergelder from destructive greed and directs the flow of his money for the public good. Part social planner, part psychological counselor, Dolly is Wilder's image of contemporary survival—getting along in this world comes through taking an imaginative chance. The expansive projects of the human spirit—adventure, playing hunches, going to New York—are what save the lives in the play.

This farce, charged with social meaning, is an altogether more modest achievement than *The Skin of Our Teeth*. The new play, which reached Broadway in wartime, is Wilder's multicolored, many-styled exploration of endurance and survival; the austerely rendered routines of Grover's Corners and the bouncy adventures of Dolly in New York both lack the craftsmanly ingenuity, the imaginative steeplechasing, and the emotional variousness of this latest three-act play. The windup-toy quality of characters like Vandergelder has also been displaced by a more satisfying and penetrating investigation of people's problems and moods.

Measuring Wilder's progress as a dramatist inevitably involves placing *The Skin of Our Teeth* beside *Our Town:* the works invite comparison not only because of their ambitiousness but more importantly because of strong thematic affinities. Both concern American families struggling with implacable fate and their own smallness: Emily and George and their parents and Mr. and Mrs. Antrobus and their children experience joy and dread as they contend not only with the localized social problems of American life, but more importantly with the churnings of the universe. The macrocosmic references in both plays—to planets, vast numbers, ideas that hover around mortal lives—are an unmistakable sign that Wilder remains obsessed by the ways ordinary

lives in Grover's Corners or Excelsior, New Jersey, take
their place in a universal design. But for all this similar-
ity in cosmic subject matter, there is a very considerable
difference in the dramatic visions of the plays. The last
act of *Our Town* takes place in a graveyard—its epiphanies are tragic, but its affirmations about stars and striving are so much inauthentic rhetoric grafted onto a great
play. Unfortunately for those who seek easy contrasts
with *The Skin of Our Teeth*, the later play—for all
its brio and broad humor—is not essentially comic, although a wide variety of comic and humorous strategies
are used in the very serious, emotionally wrenching
drama about the struggle to transcend the disasters of
nature, human society, and the warped human self. Act
III situates the family in a war-ravaged home with
Gladys as an unwed mother, Henry filled with fascistic
rage, and Sabina anxious to become a good self-absorbed
American citizen ready for a peacetime prosperity of
movies and fun. Mr. Antrobus is ready to start putting
the world together again, but he is old and tired and has
had many setbacks. This is hardly comic—and in its
matter-of-fact look at what men and women wind up
with, it is hardly the complacent vision that repelled
Mary McCarthy when she reviewed the play.[9] *The Skin
of Our Teeth* is not about the fat of the land: what's in
view for man is grinding struggle, close calls with total
destruction, and the permanent fact of human violence
and selfishness.

This theme of human struggle and limited achievement comes to us in the form of three loosely con-
structed, elliptical acts. Never a writer of well-made
plays, Wilder has now brought his own episodic technique to a pitch of dizzy perfection. From his *Journals*
we learn that Wilder considered that he was "shattering
the ossified conventions" of realistic drama in order to let
his "generalized beings" emerge.[10]

Act I, set in Excelsior, New Jersey, has about as

much logic and verisimilitude as a vaudeville skit. Using the Brechtian strategy of screen projections and announcements, Wilder surveys the "News Events of the World." Mostly the reports concern the extreme cold, the wall of ice moving south, and the scene in the home of George Antrobus. It is six o'clock and "the master not home yet"; Sabina—the sexy maid who sometimes steps out of her part to complain about the play—is parodying the chitchat that often opens a realistic well-made play: "If anything happened to him, we would certainly be inconsolable and have to move into a less desirable residential district." The dramatic movement—never Wilder's strong point—involves waiting for Antrobus, contending with the cold, disciplining a dinosaur and a mastodon, receiving Antrobus's messages about surviving ("burn everything except Shakespeare"), and living in a typical bickering American family; Maggie Antrobus—unlike her inventive, intellectual, progressive husband—is instinctual and practical. Her children, Henry and Gladys, are emblems of violence and sexuality: the boy has obviously killed his brother with a stone; the girl has trouble keeping her dress down. When their father arrives home—with a face like that of a Keystone Cop, a tendency to pinch Sabina, and a line of insults that sounds like W. C. Fields, the plot moves a bit more swiftly. He asks the dinosaur to leave and receives Homer and Moses into the house. As the act ends, the family of man is trying to conserve its ideas and knowledge —including the alphabet and arithmetic; it has also accepted "the refugees"—the Greek poet and the Hebrew lawgiver. The fire of civilization is alive, and members of the audience are asked to pass up chairs to keep it going.

Act II has the glitz of Atlantic City and the continuing problem of Mr. Antrobus dealing with the disasters of terrestrial life, the fact of his own sexuality, and the gnawing obligations of a father and husband. Once again, in the style of Brecht's epic theater, an announcer

comments on screen projections—"Fun at the Beach"
and the events of the convocation of "the Ancient and
Honorable Order of Mammals." The plot is jumpier than
ever—Miss Lily Sabina Fairweather, Miss Atlantic City
1942, tries to seduce Antrobus; a fortune-teller squawks
about coming rains; Mrs. Antrobus bickers with the children, champions the idea of the family, and protests
against Antrobus's breaking of his marriage promise;
Antrobus, ashamed of himself at last, shepherds his flock
and an assortment of animals into a boat.

Dealing with the effects of war, Act III is a powerful
ending to this play about surviving. The wild and often
inspired stage gimmickry of the first two acts has given
way to the darkened stage and the ravaged Antrobus
home. The emotions become more concentrated, the actions and efforts seem less scattered, the people's situations reach us as both tragedy and the inevitable business of men and women enduring. A play that seemed to
be in revolt against realistic character representation,
psychological probing, and the fine shadings of nineteenth-century drama, explodes into a moving exploration of personalities as they face the modern world.
Deeply affected by the suffering of the war, the family
members come into focus as human beings rather than
emblems. Henry, the linchpin of this act about war and
violence, explains himself for the first time and becomes
more than a stick figure. Resentful about having "any-
body over me" he has turned himself into a fascist as
a way of mastering the authorities—his father, especially—who oppressed him. His truculence, fierce
selfishness, and horrible individualism make him both a
believable neurotic and a distillation of brutal resentment. Sabina, the temptress who has competed with
Mrs. Antrobus for the attention of George, also comes
alive as an individual. Driven to depression and cynicism by the hardship of the war, she pronounces that
people "have a right to grab what they can find." As "just

an ordinary girl" who doesn't mind dealing in black-
market goods to pay for a night at the movies, she represents Wilder's honest appraisal of what suffering often
does to people. Antrobus—the principle of light, reason, and progress in the play—also has his moments of
depression. He yearns for simple relief: "Just a desire to
settle down; to slip into the old grooves and keep the
neighbors from walking over my lawn." But somehow a
pile of old tattered books, brought to life by passages
from Spinoza, Plato, and Aristotle delivered by stand-in
actors, rekindles the desire "to start building." Self-
interest, complacency, despair, and violence coexist
with intellectual aspirations and energies to begin again:
although outnumbered by ordinarily self-involved and
extraordinarily violent people, Antrobus can still go on.
Despite the fact that the play ends, as it began, with "the
world at sixes and sevens," there is still the principle of
the family in Mrs. Antrobus's words and the desire to
create the future from the past in Mr. Antrobus's reverence for Plato and technology.

The styles of this play are as various as modern literature and the twentieth-century stage. Not at all austere
or carefully crafted, the drama is a brilliant jumble of
Pirandello, Joyce, and epic theater.

Once again Wilder employs the manner, and the
basic outlook, of *Six Characters in Search of an Author*.
Sabina and Henry, particularly, make us aware that they
are performing, that their parts are not entirely to their
liking, and that they want to convey something about
themselves that the theater does not have the means to
express. Just as Pirandello's actors distort the story of a
tragic family, Wilder's script does not always allow Sabina to tell about her truths or Henry to explain his real-
life motivations. Like Pirandello's agonized daughter-
figure, Henry insists on the brutal truth of his situation
and interrupts the flow of the action to cry out against
the false representation that he is given by the play-

wright. The management of the stage business in *The Skin of Our Teeth* is another reminder of Pirandello's theater. The awkward, clumsy matter of props and their arrangement leads us back to *Six Characters* and its arguments about where people should stand, what a room was like, and how people should look. Wilder delights in offering us not only a drama of survival, but also the laborious process of making a play—the scaffolding of a work of art is just as much his subject as the work itself. The stops and starts, the interruptions and localized quarrels of the actors, the puncturing of the whole theatrical illusion by the reality of actors who have become sick from some food and need to be replaced: such ploys carry through Wilder's theme of struggle and endurance, but also suggest the impact of Pirandello's artfully disordered dramas. Wilder's debt to Pirandello does not end with stage technique. The vision of the play—Antrobus beginning again and the family ready "to go on for ages and ages yet"—has most often been traced to Joyce's *Finnegans Wake:* Wilder himself acknowledged this partial debt in the midst of the brouhaha about his "plagiarism" (as noted in chapter 1). Other influences were overlooked. Pirandello's tragic and tormented family in *Six Characters* goes offstage only to find another theater in which to play out its drama: in a mood of guarded optimism, this is precisely what the Antrobus family is about to do. Sabina reports that they are on their way.

The Skin of Our Teeth also becomes a more enjoyable and intelligible theatrical experience when it is placed beside Bertolt Brecht's epic-theater works. The staging, character presentation, themes, and generalizing power bear an important relationship to Brecht's experiments in the 1930s.[11] Without having to argue for direct influences, one still can see a great deal about Wilder's techniques and idea by placing them in apposition to a work like *Mother Courage*. Since both plays take place in time of war, employ epic exaggeration, ex-

plore violence and selfishness, and take an unadorned
look at what suffering does to people, it is not unreason-
able to view them together. *Mother Courage* was also
written three years before *The Skin of Our Teeth,* a fact
that is not without significance considering Wilder's
close touch with the currents of twentieth-century literature. Yet whether he was influenced directly or not, the
affinities are strong. As pieces of stagecraft, both plays
employ a large historical sweep and present material in a
nonrealistic manner; Brecht's play of the Thirty Years
War and Wilder's play of civilization's disaster both
reach for large generalizations about man's durability
and defects. The works do this essentially didactic job by
means of screen projections, announcers, jagged episodic plots, and characters who are often stereotypical or
emblematic. Wilder's third act overcomes Brecht's re-
lentless detachment from his characters, but even here
—as we sympathize with Sabina and Henry—we are
not in a theater where the individual psyche is the main
concern. Wilder is more involved with the process of
learning, the hope of progress, and the impediments in
human nature and culture than with the individuality of
his people. In this he is one with Brecht, a writer who
studies the harshness of civilization and the brutality of
ordinary folk. Sabina's selfish, compromising, essentially
amoral view of the human struggle for survival is like
nothing so much as Mother Courage's matter-of-fact attitude toward suffering and willingness to hitch up her
wagon and do business after her children are dead. Wilder has humanized and intellectualized this savage
world, but he essentially works with its terrifying ingredients. Even Antrobus, the beacon light of the three
acts, is tainted by the lust, a cynicism, cheapness, and
hypocrisy that Brecht saw as the central features of bourgeois life. While Antrobus brings his noble and selfish
impulses into a unity, he is still like Humanity as described by Brecht in *Saint Joan of the Stockyards*:

> Humanity! Two souls abide
> Within thy breast!
> Do not set either one aside:
> To live with both is best!
> Be torn apart with constant care!
> Be two in one! Be here, be there!
> Hold the low one, hold the high one—
> Hold the straight one, hold the sly one—
> Hold the pair![12]

During the period when Wilder was working on *The Skin of Our Teeth*, the influence of *Finnegans Wake* was also taking effect on his vision. In his correspondence with Edmund Wilson in 1940 and 1941 Wilder gave his own version of the Joyce connection and offered a perspective on his imagination that is more wide-ranging than Robinson and Campbell's detective work. Wilder explained to Wilson that the *Wake* was a book with "a figure in the carpet": the design, he argued, was to be discovered in Joyce's anal eroticism; the great conundrum of modern literature was all about "order, neatness, single-minded economy of means."[13] Whether or not this is a reductive interpretation of Joyce, the "discovery" tells us something about Wilder's mind, points to his own career as a preserver of other people's motifs, and suggests a possible explanation for his constant borrowings in *The Skin*. Wilder claimed that he felt a joyous "relief"[14] as he understood Joyce's psychic and literary strategies; each interpreter of these remarks (and of Wilder's *Wake* obsessions) will have to decide what they are revealing. But the present study of Wilder's imagination offers this material as another example of his loving accumulation of ideas and patterns. The letters are a way of coming to terms with his own nature.

Writing to Wilson, Wilder spoke of the *Wake* as embodying "the neurotic's frenzy to tell and not tell."[15] Tell what? the reader might ask. Once again, this remark might be turned on Wilder's own work-in-progress:

there are at least two of Wilder's recurring anxieties in the new play—resentment and guilt felt by a son *and* fear of civilization's destruction. His play, Wilder told Wilson, was meant to dramatize "the end of the world in comic strip."[16] On one level the description matched Joyce's remarks that *Finnegans Wake* is "a farce of dustiny." But Wilder's readers cannot help recalling the disaster of *The Bridge*, the end of the patrician world in *The Cabala*, the declining pagan world in *The Woman of Andros*. *The Skin of Our Teeth* may be seen as both a Joyce-burdened work and the latest version of Wilder's anxieties about violence and the collapse of Western culture.

The folk-style of *Our Town*, the social parable of *The Merchant of Yonkers*, and the rich suggestiveness and borrowing of *The Skin of Our Teeth* are three forms of expression that Wilder developed to convey the struggle of people enduring the churnings of the cosmos and the conflicts of civilization. The three plays offer guarded affirmations about man's strivings: growth and insight are abundantly available in Wilder's theater and make it altogether unlike the visions of other major American playwrights.

5

From Heaven to Newport: Two Versions of the Picaresque

George Antrobus's ingenuity and Dolly Levi's creative mother wit are a part of a larger search for coherence and progress: from the thirties onward, Wilder took leave of the essentially sterile world of the early novels and pursued a course of representing the creative impulse. His people want to believe in their ability to change the world: George Brush, the traveling Bible salesman in *Heaven's My Destination;* Julius Caesar in *The Ides of March;* John Ashley, the practical man in *The Eighth Day,* and Theophilus North in the last complete work shape their lives according to some constructive vision or code, and offer their achievements to refashion needy and often sickly societies. Strong effectual central figures dominate the post-nineteen-twenties novels and contrast—perhaps too distinctly—with Wilder's people in *The Cabala, The Bridge,* and *The Woman of Andros*. No one has ever said that the later novels are "little lavender tragedies" about perishing aesthetes. Toughened by the American Depression, by World War II and its aftermath, Wilder became the writer who responded to disaster by producing novels that explore the varieties of affirmation available to people living in settings that range from Imperial Rome to Kansas.

Two of these novels, *Heaven's My Destination*

(1935) and *Theophilus North* (1973), are picaresque surveys of the American social scene; in the first work Wilder started a new phase in his career—a departure from the aesthete's world—by plunging into a 1930s atmosphere of midwestern lunch counters, street corners, rooming houses, and camp meetings: his places seemed to have been partially colored by Edward Hopper's vision of commonplace America—a country of undramatic scenes, ordinary routines, and, as art critic Alexander Eliot has said of Hopper's work, "sights that others take for granted." But along with this honing in on moments of simple joy, boredom, and anxiety, there is also Wilder's flamboyant wit, irony, and satiric sense. The book is about George Brush, a young graduate of a Bible-belt college who is set on reforming the world and improving himself.

In satirizing Brush in *Heaven's My Destination* and reporting on the colors and moods of 1931, Wilder succeeded in producing another of his best blendings of styles—the work is deft and gentle and at the same time filled with piquant insight into the American character. In 1973, Wilder again offered a story of a young man who goes around giving advice and mending destinies. Cast into a series of loosely related episodes, *Theophilus North* is also the tale of the picaro as do-gooder; this time, however, Wilder has changed his protagonist from a theorizer and woolly idealist to an artist and conjurer. The two books are two views of men facing human misery and achieving some conquests through will, strength and ingenuity. Wilder, the writer who chronicled failure in the twenties, looked for some ways out of the cycle of suffering in these books: in both cases he used the comic mode.

Although *Heaven's My Destination* offers a highly caricatured central character, minor people who are often cartoonlike, and emotional scenes with no more depth than vaudeville acts, it manages to hold the reader's attention because of its ironic balance of elements, its fast-paced plot, and its authentic atmosphere. The plot line is no more ingenious and artful than the typical picaresque work—its reason for being is to show Brush as a relentlessly idealistic innocent colliding with Babbitts, farm girls, and salesmen. The episodes are as predictable and broad as a comic strip, but they are also given charm and ironic significance as Wilder selects the sharp detail or the incongruous situation to highlight his protagonist's naïveté. Each chapter is headed by a brief description of the contents, a strategy that adds the flavor of the eighteenth-century novel to a twentieth-century American book about an isolated progressive. Wilder—always the writer who experimented with mixing tones—makes the chapters into amalgams of roughhouse and didactic reflection: typically, the plot deals with George's gaffes, misfired good intentions, and theories about human conduct that derail when they are acted on. With a headful of Gandhi's pacificism, evangelicism, and assorted information from the *Encyclopaedia Britannica,* George sets out to right the wrongs of the world. After a hundred and fifty pages of doing the right thing—reasoning with burglars, telling women not to smoke, comforting small children, helping traumatized people to regain their balance—George loses his missionary zeal as a result of a failed marriage. If he cannot be a happy family man, he might as well cheat on his expense account, forget to say his prayers, laugh loudly in the movies—and collapse.

Wilder makes each chapter into an occasion for exhibiting George as a spectacle of misplaced faith and misdirected benevolence. A clumsy dispenser of abstract ideas as he deals with down-to-earth types, he generally makes a show of himself and gets a beating, a tongue lashing, or a night in jail. Wilder has avoided the danger of this kind of plot—the sheer monotony of the episodic structure—by concocting mistakes that draw

attention to the gap between wild, ideal schemes and
practical problems: while George is off on some spiritual
flight, the midwestern people who surround him are
pursuing their literal-minded way through the Depression. Isolation—almost always a Wilder theme—is now
subject matter for comedy.

George Brush's pratfalls give whatever shape there
is to the plot: doing good and following his best social impulses amounts to refusing to play along with cheating,
profit-making, and unchristian living. As George refuses
to accept interest from the bank, to oppose criminals
with violence, and to assert himself aggressively, he
finds his friends turn on him and strangers have him ar-
rested. Chapter 1 shows him spending a night in jail for
explaining his queer theories of economics to a baffled
bank official. In each chapter he continues to be crazily
conscientious and kind. Using courtesies on tarts and
modern psychology on thieves, he winds up as a spectacle. In the end, after being buffeted and rejected by less-
reflective people, he falls apart: nothing has come of all
his theories, experiments, and good instincts. His major
ambition—to be a father in an "American Home"—has
fallen to pieces after his farm-girl wife leaves him; he has
driven his friends to violence and rage. But as the narrative closes, George pulls himself together and sets off on
another mission—offering to send waitresses to college.

George Brush himself is far more radical than Wilder's other protagonists: after writing about victims and
passive receptors of modern culture, Wilder has created
an activist and do-gooder whose vigor and ingenuity
make Dolly Levi seem lethargic. A man of his time intellectually, George is a restless, often annoying theorizer
who likes to work out benign schemes—even if he
upends the lives of those around him. He combines his
social subversiveness with an endearing old-fashioned
belief in love, friendliness, and family. Too ironically
portrayed and too dizzy to be sappy, George comes off

altogether differently from sentimental positive thinkers and other sunny reformers. He is essentially a Quixote who cannot be humbled, a Candide who refuses to see anything bad enough to make him cultivate his own garden. Meddling and wondering how life can be better is his joyous vocation.

The other characters in the novel tend to be skillfully rendered stick figures who serve as foils for Brush. There is Doremus Blodgett, salesman for the Everlast Hosiery Company, and his friend and drinking pal Margie McCoy. The latter "had a large puffy face heavily covered with powder. It was surmounted by a fine head of orange, brown, and black hair." These two can't believe Brush's benevolent antics and sententiousness: their dialogue, along with the broad brush strokes that describe their appearance, rings true and carries a characteristic Wilder theme. Margie's response to George is just about what everyone else will tell him:

You make me sick. Where do they get yuh, your the'ries and your ideas? Nowhere? Live, kid,—live! What'd become of all of us sons-a-bitches, if we stopped to argue out every step we took? Stick down to earth.

The message—a warning against the dangers of idealism—clearly connects George's problems with those of Wilder's protagonists in the 1920s novels: the self-absorption of theorizers and obsessive types—whether Blair in *The Cabala*, or the Marquesa in *The Bridge*—is life-denying and, as Margie McCoy puts it, "only makes you twice as blue." George, like the characters in earlier novels, finds that the world will not adjust to his vision: but unlike those essentially tragic and pathetic types, he has the resilience of a comic character. His comic worth comes from his pursuit of ideals in a fallen world; like the suffering in *The Bridge*, this pursuit is not without value—in the end it produces an enduring energy that keeps Brush going. Although tormented with depression and rejection, he does not fall into madness, despair, or self-destruction like the people in the early books.

But for all George's energy, he is not like the sub-lime good people in modern literature. He once ruined a girl, and he often gets caught up in situations that make him harm others. His innocence is ironically tarnished by human instincts and also by what Wilder perceives as the essentially faulty precepts of Protestant evangeli-cism.[1] Never quite reaching a higher realization of what the world's evil is all about, he remains ignorant. In this he is unlike another holy fool of our time—Isaac Ba-shevis Singer's Gimpel. Calling the insights of this char-acter to mind—especially his recognition that lying holds the social order together—makes the reader real-ize that George Brush, for all his spiritual drive and kindness, is incapable of seeing the larger pattern of worldly evil. Like Gimpel the Fool, he scurries around trying to make people decent; but unlike Gimpel, he never achieves much insight into the casual indecency of modern life. There is also, regrettably, no clear evidence that Wilder saw the disorder of his times with any de-gree of clarity. Pushing forward to affirmations, he cre-ated a character who seems to be grappling with less in-sidious problems than those presented in the 1920s novels. Although Wilder felt the book was "in every paragraph a Depression novel,"[2] the reader is likely to find George's misadventures more memorable than the vision of a nation in economic chaos. More skilled at ridiculing the qualities of his picaro than at exploring the depths of American suffering, Wilder did not connect George's dizzy thinking with the general state of the country.

But even though *Heaven's My Destination*—with the cartoon characters and conflicts—may not be a con-frontation with the disorder of the 1930s, it is an extraor-dinary work of American landscape painting. A veritable gallery of native scenes, the book sticks in the mind as a

loving and ironic report on how people lived during the
Depression. Wilder's special strategy involved humor,
incongruity, and a keen eye for the worn and seedy quality of many American places; using a plain technique
that removed all the adornment and elaborate scene
painting of the 1920s novels, Wilder presented midwestern life in the unromantic colors and simple forms of the
realist. Written some eight years before *Our Town,* this
novel had a completely different approach to atmosphere: Wilder's gift for connecting the ingredients of
ordinary lives with the cosmic order was not as yet
developed; instead, the narrative of George Brush is im-
planted in the particulars of city and rural life. What is
universal, flattened out, and rendered in the style of the
folk artist in *Our Town* is given specific texture and the
grain and tone of our most interesting realistic painters
in *Heaven's My Destination.* Look, for example, at Wilder's eye for American juxtapositions. (George, the innocent, is sent as a Sunday caller to a brothel in Kansas
City run by Ma Crofut.) "If it had any faults at all, it was
that the paint lacked freshness and that it was too closely
hemmed in by a business college on one side and an undertaking establishment on the other." The landscaping
of this house is another example of Wilder's deft, ironic
brush stroke: "For some reason a dilapidated electric
sign board lay half hidden in the rhododendron bushes;
it said: The Riviera. Cuisine Francaise."

Readers who somehow feel Wilder is too genteel
should look at his scene in Queenie Cravet's Kansas City
boardinghouse:

Most of the doors had long been smashed, and after lying about
as boards had finally disappeared in smaller and smaller fragments. Several partitions between the rooms contained holes,
opened up in some historic rough house, and now offering the
testimony of their splintering edges and crumbling plaster. A
smell floated about, made of of foul clothes, antiseptic soap,
gin, and lemon peel.

There is more of the feel of the Reginald Marsh painting in such a description than Wilder's proletarian detractors will allow.

The scenes deserve special attention because of their combination of clear detail, honesty, and wit. Never the dour naturalist painting squalor, Wilder nevertheless knows how to tell the truth about ordinary life. To this truth he always adds a bit of playfulness. George Brush approaches an apartment house in Fort Worth, Texas, where one tenant has signs for "Spiritualistic Readings" and "Varicose Veins Reduced." On another occasion in Kansas City he searches for the girl he once slept with and checks The Rising Sun Chop Suey Palace. The waitresses . . .

were dressed in a vaguely Chinese costume that included red satin trousers. A disc of rouge had been drawn on each cheek and their eyebrows had been painted in an upward curve at the outer edges.

The atmosphere comes alive when George asks "a tall long girl with a mass of dishevelled hair and a sullen expression" about the best dishes. "Everyone of 'm 'll give you a great big thrill you'll never forget."

Heaven's My Destination was Wilder's first full-scale breakthrough into the American idiom. As a comic-ironic survey of our country and of our Protestant impulse to do good, the book has a special place in American letters. Without the pretentiousness of Sinclair Lewis or the noisiness of H. L. Mencken, Wilder made his mark as an incisive observer of midwestern manners. Too playful to hold people up to savage ridicule and too serious to find an audience looking for lightweight entertainment, Wilder missed the more easily accepted fictional categories. But if readers of our time go to *Heaven's My Destination* for wit and vivid scenes that embody American absurdity, they will find George Brush amid the clutter of American popular culture. In this early work, Wilder, if nothing else, broke out of his tendency to use the novel form for an examination of the special consciousness.

While *Heaven's My Destination* is rapidly narrated and economical, Wilder's next use of the picaresque mode, *Theophilus North,* is an overblown and often self-indulgent production. Written when Wilder was in his seventies, the book looks backward; but, as a survey of Wilder's strategies in his fiction will easily show, Wilder's general tendency had been to look elsewhere—out of himself to Peru, to ancient Rome, and to the Bible belt that he knew from a lecture tour. *Theophilus North* is essentially about being young, being ingenious, being resourceful, and being Thornton Wilder. The fictive disguise that Wilder gives himself is very thin and the episodes have the overly detailed quality that comes from remembering exactly how things looked and felt, rather than from establishing what they meant. While George Brush is a character seen at a distance and created from a few dominant traits, Theophilus North—speaking in his own voice—explains himself fully but not clearly to the reader. He claims to be another of Wilder's role players —perhaps like Uncle Pio: like the earlier character, he tries to assume the duties of man of the world, thinker, spy, sometime scholar, and lover of the arts. But Theophilus' schemes and visions finally make the book come off as a strained replay of old Wilder motifs. Here the reader can see the dangers of Wilder's imitative strategy: things go well until the author starts recalling his own success.

On the surface, the affinities between *Theophilus North* and *Heaven's My Destination* are difficult to ignore. Both novels are the adventures of earnest young men, modern knights errant in search of injustices and wrongs; their variously heavy and light-handed meddlings constitute the plots. George Brush's methods are the old-fashioned Protestant preachments and good

works that have their origins in the Calvinism of Amos
Wilder; Theophilus North's approach is the playful assuming of guises, the adopting of roles to show people
new images of themselves. Typically, he will stage a
scene—say, pretend to teach French when he is teaching mature behavior to a teenager. Both novels have
Wilder's post-nineteen-twenties wit and irony, although
the later work loses the taut and brisk quality of George's
story because of its occasional descents into sentimentality and didacticism. But *Theophilus*, for all its faults, has
one quality that sets it apart from *Heaven*—a much
firmer and more mature grasp of the problem of man-
made obstacles, injustices, and limitations on freedom.
If Freud had lived to read the new novel, he certainly
would have pronounced it an advance, in its vision of the
troubled human psyche, on *Heaven's My Destination*. In
fact, Wilder infused certain key insights of Freudian psychology with a charming and liberating wit that Freud
himself would have considered a heroic struggle against
misery. Wilder's protagonist becomes a man who will
not submit to the world of repressed and neurotic types
at Newport: he uses humorous ploys as his forms of practical therapy.

The plot of *Theophilus North* is actually a series of
visits made by our protagonist to the homes of psychologically and socially troubled people. Instead of making
tours of the great houses in Newport, Theophilus journeys through Newport's "Nine Cities"—from patrician
homes to those of the nouveau riche and then the working people—and uncovers, in the manner of the archae-
ologist-cum-psychoanalyst, the illnesses that appear to
the rest of the world as either mysteries or eccentrici-
ties. The young man who does the touring and healing
starts out with nine ambitions: to be a saint, an anthro-
pologist, an archaeologist, a detective, an actor, a magician, a lover, a rascal, and a free man. The last role offers
the key to the book: for in each episode Theophilus pro-

tects himself from restraining allegiances, conventional jobs, and entangling relationships. Like the classic psychoanalyst—a role that he avoids mentioning, but that radiates off "detective" and "archaeologist"—he studiously tries to avoid getting personal and therefore retains his healing powers. In order to make a living and preserve a measure of freedom, he hires himself out as a tutor and reader. The answers that he gets to his advertisements are like so many calls for help; the people whom he meets—even those not connected with his work—are Newport's neediest; the functions that he performs for them—all in the course of tutoring French or reading aloud—would daunt even Dolly Levi. He mitigates or brings understanding to the following troubles, illnesses and injustices: pride of rank, haunted houses, aristocratic loneliness, oversensitivity, adolescent snobbishness, prudery, isolation, childlessness, migraine headaches, and class restrictions. If all this sounds as if Theophilus has in fact assumed the role of magician, that is because Wilder does not mind comic exaggeration and playful attempts to deal with the broad range of human unhappiness. Surprisingly enough in a story with so many cures and improvements effected by one man, *Theophilus North* is not a matter of silly wish fulfillments and infantile dreams of conquest. Theophilus' brains, intuition, mother wit, and humor are the sources of humane progress. He is a realistic and rather tough-minded analyst of his fellows' troubles—drawing away from conventional pity and sympathy, he tries to put his clients in the position to observe their lives and live. Like a good doctor, his compassion takes the form of useful strategies rather than idle advice.

The episodes are sparkling, often deftly handled treatments of various human predicaments; but regrettably, the problems that "Ted" faces often involve characters who fail to come to life on the page. Wilder's afflicted people—the latest group of neurotics created by

the writer who studied warped lives in *The Cabala* and
The Bridge—seem to be curable, but also appear before
us as textureless and rather transparent cases. Getting
involved with the conflicts and identities of these figures
is not easy. Dr. James McHenry Bosworth, for example,
is an elderly patrician who lives in an exquisitely ap-
pointed cottage called "Nine Gables," a remnant of
eighteenth-century Newport. This highly cultivated and
philosophical man is imprisoned in his own home by an
overbearing daughter who has caused him to lose his
confidence and fall prey to fears about his health. In an
atmosphere filled with John Singer Sargent portraits and
platoons of servants, poor Bosworth tries to work on a
plan for a philosophical institute to be founded in
Newport. The only aspect of Bosworth's dilemma that is
interesting is Wilder's cleverness in handling the relationships between Dr. Bosworth's health problem—a
weak bladder—and his favorite philosopher—Bishop
Berkeley. Theophilus, through several comic strategies,
cures the old man of the problem—which, like Berkeley's material world, is all in the head. But such farcical
doings never succeed in making Bosworth more than a
stereotypical old swell.

Sometimes Wilder's wit and dramatic sense succeed in giving the illusion of character depth. In the
chapter called "The Fenwicks," Theophilus is summoned to deal with a very snobbish teenage boy who pa-
tronizes his family and friends and is obsessed with Yale
societies and family background. Theophilus finds these
affectations to be related to fears of the human body and
ordinariness. To cure his pupil he puts him through a
very funny course of imaginary interviews: Theophilus,
the French tutor, and his student assume parts in little
playlets about Parisian life. The young boy learns how to
be polite and unpretentious in his dealing with a French
tart. Such "make believe is like a dream—escape, release." It charms the reader into believing that the boy is

more than a stick figure. But the small dramatic scene should also remind us of a familiar Wilder ploy: in *Childhood* the children go on a "bus ride" to learn what their parents are all about; and back as far as *The Bridge*, Wilder has Uncle Pio discovering his feelings in fictional situations and through assuming guises.

Theophilus North is quite explicit in its use of conjuring, pretending, and fictionalizing as the paths to truth and happiness.[3] There is scarcely a chapter that does not have Theophilus designing scenes, assuming roles, and maneuvering people into play-acting and taking on imaginary identities. The book, despite its old-fashioned portraiture, is intensely modern in its presentation of the collision of artifice and life. True to his bookish vision, Wilder devises scenes where fantasies and literary works are the central features. Two of the best episodes show Theophilus the artificer creating a delightful order in the lives of troubled people by using fiction and trickery to overcome obstacles. In the chapter called "The Wyckoff Place," our protagonist goes to a Palladian-style cottage as a reader and hears a story about the bad reputation that has bedeviled the Wyckoff house because of a nineteenth-century scandal. It seems that the present owner's father left the house on a trip and came home to find his servants had taken over the place for a night of orgiastic revels; the rumors about the scandal finally wound up as spook stories in the next generation. The predicament at the house is a bit of plot material that Wilder lifted wholesale from his own early play *The Trumpet Shall Sound*. But this time, instead of having a master who returns to bring order and set his household to rights, Wilder uses Theophilus the detective-public-relations man: since rumor is made up of stories based on isolated facts, Theophilus decides to rehabilitate the house's reputation by embroidering stories about the artistic reputation of the Wyckoff place; he makes a contract with Newport's best gossip colum-

nist—and tricks her into thinking that she's getting a
great scoop on life in a house of distinction; the story
that she writes embroiders on his initial fictions. Miss
Wyckoff, the distressed owner, recaptures the beauty of
her childhood as the malodorous reputation vanishes;
she prepares to entertain guests with an evening of
Mozart, and learns to accept Theophilus' philosophy of
order: the world—as Dolly Levi once said—needs to be
adjusted to our dreams of joy; if lying will do the job,
why not? Now the distance that separates Theophilus'
world of artifice from idle daydreaming is quite considerable. Theophilus the creator and inventor is altogether
different from the neurotic fantasizers of the early novels. As he scurries through the lives in Newport's Nine
Cities, he becomes a doer of deeds, a fabricator whose
artistic impulses have the healing and cathartic powers
that thinkers from Aristotle to Freud have assigned
to the creative mind. Theophilus' inventions—like
Wilder's—are, in Aristotle's formulation, truer than history because they deal with the universal desires of the
human heart.

The restorative powers of art and humorous designing give substance to chapters that are otherwise un-
distinguished: a typical example is the section called
"Myra," the story of a depressed rich woman who is in-
valided during pregnancy and forced to fall back on a
course of daily reading. Theophilus is called in to interest Myra in books—heretofore she has been a Shake-
speare-hating philistine—and also to keep her pacified
while her husband is pursuing an affair with a French
woman. But no sooner does our Ted introduce his young
client to the English novel and Shakespeare than she
changes from a listless and literal-minded bore to a
forceful and imaginative woman. The transformation
comes about when Theophilus introduces Myra to
Shakespeare's romantic heroines—Viola, Rosalind, Imo-
gene—and their "humorous minds." These women tran-

scend the circumstances of an oppressive male-domi-
nated society by using disguises and wit. Theophilus
tells Myra that their strategies, paradoxically, help them
to confront "the real." As a result, "They're never
crushed or shocked or at their wit's end." Myra takes the
lecture to heart and dresses up in pants like Shakespeare's ladies and her husband's emancipated mistress.
Her trick helps her out of her own depression and rouses
her husband into taking a better look at himself. Contrived as all this seems as plot material, it comes across
as a charming parable about imagination and its power to
mitigate human suffering. Myra and her husband are
uninspired creations, but Wilder's Theophilus and his
playful missionary work almost make them vibrate with
the joy of discovering the humor and creative energy of
the world.

When we measure Theophilus' action against those
of Samuele, the protagonist of *The Cabala,* we see how
far Wilder had come in representing the human being
facing the pain of neurosis. Both the first and last novels
are about young men who enter exclusive communities
only to find the victims of the class system suffering
mightily and genteely in brocaded drawing rooms; Wilder's ironic sense and unfailingly beautiful style raise
both novels many powers above trite stories about the
miserable rich. But whereas Samuele is a shadowy, in-
substantial character who makes nothing happen among
the fascinating Roman grotesques—an observer who
seems not even to learn much, Theophilus is a well-
drawn, active, imaginative, and effectual character who
animates the novel and propels its dull people. Wilder
has given his best energies to his protagonist in this last
work; Theophilus becomes a kind of spokesman for wit,
joy, and the ordering powers of the imagination. But
here again there is something lacking, a withholding of
intimacy that once made Samuele shadowy and that now
makes Theophilus essentially distant and unreachable as

a character. Like Wilder himself—the friendly teacher who remained at a distance, the frank and forthright man whose ambiguous and veiled attitude toward his private life is so much a feature of his career—Theophilus is not especially accessible. In the book's conclusion, Theophilus orchestrates a great Servants' Ball in Newport at which the help and the gentry all meet on friendly terms. But after all the planning and scurrying and imaginative creation, he himself watches the occasion from a nearby house. Wilder, the writer who could transport us to eighteenth-century Peru without ever having been there, performed his last trick in *Theophilus North:* he wrote an autobiographical picaresque novel without revealing anything about himself as a man.[4] While the artist and conjurer has planned the world of Newport, the man looks at the production from a distance.

Wilder left *Theophilus North* as a final flawed symbol of his literary identity; it is a book of protean transformations, disguises, role-playing, and ironic withdrawal. As his second experiment with the picaresque mode— so different in its themes, characters, and setting from *Heaven's My Destination*—it shares the first novel's playfulness and irony: both books deal with the comic consequences that develop as their protagonists attempt to shape a more orderly world. But while *Heaven's My Destination* exposes George Brush's theorizing nature to clear light of Wilder's gentle ridicule, *Theophilus North* leaves us with an essentially mysterious central character whose imaginative nature creates role after role and finally gives the reader the slip.

6

Floating in the
Teleological Tide:
The Late Philosophical Novels

Wilder's picaresque narratives explore artifice and direct playful irony on the inquiring, rational mind. But his most profound handling of the large questions on his own agenda—destiny, causation, pain, man being measured against the universe—are to be found in novels with meditative tones and unhurried, sustained portrayals of people. *Heaven's My Destination* and *Theophilus North* bristle with ideas, but they also light upon Wilder's themes in a random way. For concentrated power, depth of analysis, and range of emotions, his two most ambitious novels are *The Ides of March* and *The Eighth Day*. Like the 1920s novels, they explore man's destiny and the mainsprings of human action; they also take on the mysteries of suffering and the troubled depths of people who are pushed to their limit. Unlike *The Cabala* and *The Bridge*, these new explorations are not easily accessible, sleekly presented, or proportioned to suit the general taste. For better or worse, they involve challenges and obstacles that the Wilder reader is unaccustomed to: the early novels offered ideas and emotions in delicately inlaid chapters; these new books often seem unevenly patterned, bumpy, awkward, and a bit repetitious. The reader who is used to the mandarin style of *The Bridge* or the tight-lipped folksiness of *Our Town* has to get used to a late philosophical style that searches for truths through talk, letters, and long meditations. Lacking swiftness and drama, these novels analyze and muse.

The *Ides of March* is a curiosity of twentieth-century literature: it is an epistolary novel, a historical evocation, a fantasia, and a series of discourses.[1] Divided into four books that cover and re-cover the last year of Julius Caesar's life, the narrative form is complicated by an odd use of repetition. Wilder, the writer who plays with time and history in *The Skin of Our Teeth* and the short one-act plays, has devised a new way of forcing us to attend to man's relationship to the temporal order by moving across the same period in sections that take in longer and longer stretches of Caesar's life. The structure could be represented visually by lines (corresponding to Books I, II, III, and IV) that are longer to denote the extended time frame. Book I covers September 45 B.C.; Book II begins earlier and ends in October. Book III begins earlier still and extends to December; the final book goes farther back and extends forward in time to end with Caesar's assassination in March 44 B.C. The effect of this extension and retroversing of one period is to make the reader feel all the currents that swirled around Caesar and all the different lives that touched his. No single story, Caesar's life becomes a series of retellings presented in letters exchanged by historians, the poet Catullus, his friends, and political opponents.

Book I concerns September 45 B.C. and the major conflicts in Caesar's mental life—his religious skepticism and his distrust of "the enemies of order, especially malcontents like Clodius Pulcher and men like Cicero who are more fond of discourse than deeds." Caesar emerges in this long section as a man in search of liberating action, one whose reflections are not so much philosophical as practical—to find his place within the scheme of the universe is his only task as a thinker. What

Rome has become—a city of flatterers, profligates, and aesthetes—is dramatically opposed to his austere conception of service, personal destiny, and work. Another of Wilder's builders—like Mr. Antrobus at the beginning of the 1940s and John Ashley in the 1960s—Wilder's Caesar opposes the forces of chaos—whether fanaticism, neurotic self-involvement, or ideological obsession. The first Book of *The Ides* makes Caesar seem like an existentialist tyrant, a dictator who takes it as his rule of life that philosophizing is less important than living.[2] Like the existentialists, Caesar muses on the necessity for defending one's being through lonely, responsible action—"the more decisions that you are forced to make alone, the more you are aware of your freedom to choose." As he rules and shapes Rome according to his conception of harmony, order, and virtue, he chooses to become the enemy of others and therefore seals his own destiny. By the concluding pages of Book I, the first attempt has been made on Caesar's life.

While Book I focuses on choice and freedom, Book II explores the idea of love and the reality of a number of erotic relationships. Cleopatra—before her entrance in October and thereafter—is the most gossiped-about character in Roman correspondences. To many women she is vulgar, dangerously ambitious, and likely to destabilize Roman politics. Her son Caesarion is Caesar's child, and the Queen has come to Rome to establish his claims. Many patrician women see her as a barbarian, a pretentious Easterner who brings corruption to the city. This surface characterizing is counterpointed by Caesar's correspondence. Book II comes alive as an emotional experience when we listen to Caesar's passionate but ambivalent responses: he is drawn to her beauty and intelligence, her conversation and exoticism; and yet he is fearful that she is another of the enemies of order. Caesar's love becomes powerful and complex as it alternates between feeling for a woman and devotion to Roman or-

der and progress. This section ends as Cleopatra begins
her Roman escapades with Marc Antony: she is caught in
a romantic situation with Caesar's nephew, and this betrayal of Caesar becomes a foreshadowing of his eventual
betrayal by others. Meanwhile, the themes of futility
and the pain of love—so vital to *The Bridge*—have been
threaded through the letters of Book II: Clodia Pulcher,
notorious sister of the Roman plotter and profligate,
Caesar's former mistress, is shown in her role as tormen-
tor of the poet Catullus. Like the Perichole in *The
Bridge*, Clodia is self-destructive and her "passionate hatred of life" leads her to the kind of sadistic truths that
can be traced back to Wilder's involvement with the
models of Proust's faithless women. Catullus, however,
is more than the wounded artist: his recognition about
his fate is precisely what we have found in the concluding pages of *The Bridge*—while Clodia has brought pain
and destruction, she has nevertheless animated her
lover and helped to create the substance of his poetry:
"By you I know that love exists." Expressing his state in
Platonic terms, Catullus says that "God Eros descended
upon me. I was more than myself." This idea of transcendence reaches back to the 1920s and the recognitions of
all the people in *The Bridge*: Wilder, always the artist
who calculates the tragic costs of emotional involvement,
insists that commitment and pain are ennobling. Cytheris, a Roman actress who has been betrayed by Marc
Antony, is yet another character in this exploration of romantic disaster. Saved from sentimentality and soap-
opera philosophizing by the sharp, often abrupt style of
the letters, Book II of *The Ides* achieves artistic poise
and ironic vision because of the remarks of those who
cannot understand deep involvement. Wilder's Cicero,
for example, is presented as a misogynistic prig who discourses to his friend Atticus on the weakness and triviality of women. His totally simplistic psychology of woman's nature—complete with remarks about women as

the enemies of civilization and progress—only serves to highlight complex women like Cleopatra and Cytheris; the absurd rhetoric—not unfamiliar to the Wilder reader who remembers the slurs on Mrs. Antrobus and her sensible concerns and domestic absorption—is here used for the purpose of showing all the nonsense that goes by the name of philosophizing. The experience of love in the lives of Catallus, Caesar, and Cleopatra—with its torment and its transcendent dimensions—is much more convincing to the reader than Cicero's rantings.

The ostensible subject matter of Book III is religion, particularly the circumstances that surround the ceremony of the Good Goddess: this Roman observance concerns women, fertility, and the welfare of the home. Its nature is shrouded in mystery; it is rumored to contain sexual license and obscenity. The direction of Book III goes from talk about preparations to a catastrophic episode in which Clodia Pulcher pollutes the rites by introducing her brother dressed as a woman. Structurally, this offense against Roman piety is another piece of foreshadowing and it helps to establish our sense that Caesar's world of dignity and restraint is rapidly disintegrating. The book also contains Caesar's further musings, continued from Book I, on the nature of his place in Roman religion: with no desire to become a god or object of veneration, he protests against the superstition of his fellow citizens. A humanist in his belief in rational choice, man's limitations, and the ruler's paradoxical strength in weakness, he presides over a state in which various fanatacisms and obsessions are beginning to overwhelm the polity. Wilder uses the religious subject matter as a springboard to explore a question that is much more pressing in this book and that has its roots in *The Bridge of San Luis Rey:* the metaphysics of hope and yearning. Hardened by war and the practice of statecraft, Caesar feels that there is a large field that "our longing cannot

alter and which our fears cannot forefend." But out of
this firm belief he does not derive the stoicism of his
contemporaries—the world is not a matter of the "variety of human endeavor and unsubstantiality of life's
joys." Caesar rejects ordinary resignation as firmly as he
rejected superstition: in its place he deals with "the inevitable" by collaborating with it rather than submitting. "I
not only bow to the inevitable, I am fortified by it. The
achievements of men are more remarkable when one
contemplates the limitations under which they labor."
This belief leads him to a way of surveying the world that
is like that of the last pages of *The Bridge:* in the early
work the bridge of love was the discovery made after
chapters of enduring pain and accident and disaster; the
informing principle of Caesar's life is not far from that
discovery. "At the closer range we say *good* and *evil*, but
what the world profits by is intensity." This new name
for the spiritual charge put on the world by men of hope
—not love, but intensity—doesn't do much to alter
Wilder's resolution in *The Bridge:* but it comes in the
life of a powerful protagonist who is far beyond the desolate world of the early novels. While Caesar too must
soon die, he has found more to praise and rejoice in than
the Marquesa or the others in *The Bridge*. Once said,
however, this should not obscure that fact that Book III
of *The Ides* is about a man who has built a personal fortress against desolation; in this he is like the Marquesa
and her great letter about courage.

The concluding Book IV picks up the thread of this
theme of courage and carries it to the very brink of disaster in March. The tension mounts as broadsides against
the dictator are circulated. Without panic, despair, or
the ordinary man's vengefulness, Caesar prepares himself for his fate—and even reasons that if he were not
Caesar he would be Caesar's assassin. Completely un-
sentimental in treating Caesar's encounter with his own
mortality and vulnerability, Wilder chooses instead to

make his protagonist an existential struggler who tries to puzzle out his own moods and his attitudes about existence as they alternate between a sense of the void and a sense of life's harmony and pleasure. The "terror in the mind"—much like what Tolstoy's Levin felt as he faced his own inconsequence in *Anna Karenina*—is the "counterpoint" of "the unspeakable happiness and confidence" that he feels during his epileptic fits. In the total existential picture, neither experience can be dismissed as an illusion. Like Emily in *Our Town*, Caesar, the most powerful man of his time, is also seized by a great feeling for the trivial details of life: "our lives are immersed in the trivial; the significant comes to us enwrapped in multitudinous details of the trivial; the trivial has this dignity that it exists and is omnipresent." The Roman dictator and the young girl in Grover's Corners share the sense that the world's meaning is packaged in the most ordinary routines and objects. Both face the reality of death—one at the Senate, one in New Hampshire—as they encounter the dignity of the ordinary. Both are filled with a sense of life's possibility as they face their own insignificance.

The texture of *The Ides of March* is perhaps its most remarkable feature—not quite a historical novel, it is instead the fantasia that Wilder called it.[3] Relieved of the duties of scholarly accuracy—or even the verisimilitude that requires the historical novelist to avoid anachronism and reading into characters' lives—Wilder can range freely among modern ideas and ancient personalities, often blending the two in strange ways. It is unlikely, for example, that Julius Caesar ever phrased the problem of freedom and fate in the language of Jean-Paul Sartre: the seeming inappropriateness of imposing the vocabulary of existentialism on a Roman military genius nevertheless is overcome as Wilder shows us that Caesar and Rome are pretexts for general speculations; no more scrupulous about accuracy than he was with stage logic in his

plays, Wilder has here made Rome another of his fabulous sets and Caesar another protagonist being tested by
agony and personal mission. Malcolm Cowley's incisive
remarks about Wilder's kind of fiction help locate the
precise nature of the *Ides:* he elucidates Wilder's imagination by pointing us in the direction of the *contes phi-
losophiques*—Voltaire's fictive discourses on problems
of thought.[4] Like *Candide* in its use of Leibniz, *The Ides*
feeds off a contemporary philosophical school and ad-
justs ideas for its own purposes.

Wilder is certainly not a committed existentialist
and his novel displays the ideas of the school in a much
looser and stranger way than would an obvious novelistic
proponent like Camus.[5] There is a curious blending of
resources that causes Caesar to be part existentialist,
part mover of world affairs, and part endurer. In assuming the last role, Caesar becomes Wilder's original creation and stands in an important relationship to other
Wilder characters. He is like Uncle Pio in his breadth of
experience, depth of suffering, and commitment to a life
of action and involvement. He also feels kinship with
artists—in this case Catullus—because the artist, like
the statesman, must make constant decisions. Who can
advise either on "that unbroken succession of choices"
that constitutes a policy or a poem? Caesar is isolated
with "the obligation to create, moment by moment," his
own Rome. By creating like the artist, he becomes a figure who completes a question raised in Wilder's first
novel, *The Cabala*—how to make a world of meaning
from the rubble of human weaknesses. Wilder's Caesar
—although troubled by doubt, the perhaps careless
working of destiny, and the hatred and flattery of his
contemporaries—is an emblem of fortitude who stands
up to disaster by resolute action. Nothing could be farther from Wilder's early indecisive people; this latest
protagonist—equipped with the philosophical resources
of the existentialists—has committed himself to "the

first and last schoolmaster of life"—"living and committing oneself unreservedly and dangerously to living."

Amazingly enough, the welter of ideas and adaptations in *The Ides of March* leaves the vitality of the characters undamaged. Novelists of ideas are always in danger of destroying their people by burying them in a morass of talk or cultural atmosphere: although *The Ides* is exceptionally talky, indeed even gossipy, the people emerge clearly and passionately. Wilder's strategy for lifting them out of the mass of letters and journals is to make them, once again, individualized victims of history and destiny. Ignoring the nuts and bolts of the ordinary historical novel, Wilder highlights moments of pain and gives a central place to injured identities. One character in the book, Lucius Manilius Turrinus, is a severely disabled general of Caesar's, once tortured by the Belgians, whom Wilder informs with the traits of his playwright friend Edward Sheldon.[6] The dedication to Sheldon —"who though immobile and blind for more than twenty years, was the dispenser of wisdom, courage, and gaiety to a large number of people"—directs us to a character who makes the novel altogether more profound in its exploration of pain than are *The Cabala* and *The Bridge*. Turrinus is not one of the letter writers in the book—and therefore we do not actually hear his voice; but his personal charm and strength cause his friends to develop insights as they communicate with him. Just as Wilder told Sheldon of his anxieties about his plays, Caesar confides his deepest fears and hopes to his old fellow campaigner. Turrinus is credited by Caesar with instilling his commander with the idea of the "Inevitable Occasion"—the phrase covering all the limitations of human life, the most obvious of which is death. Without Turrinus's situation as the isolated suffering victim, the effectiveness of such passages would be considerably diminished. The section in Book IV, on facing the void, a long passage in which Caesar measures his

dreams (of nothingness and of human achievement) de-
rives its power from the fact that Caesar, the existential
hero, has given meaning to his own life through the
Rome he has envisioned, just as Turrinus has placed his
imprint on Roman society through his wit, courage, and
wise counsel.

Wilder's characters achieve significance as they
strain to define the limits of their freedom: Catullus, in
his striving to rise above the injury of love into a realm of
transcendent order, is one of the most memorable. In
Wilder's version, he is another victim—a creator who
has resisted the painful terms of his existence while feeding off them. Clodia—clearly thinking of her lover
—describes his nature by saying that "the world of poets
is the creation not of deeper insights but of more urgent
longings." The scorn they pour on life, because of their
suffering, is done "in such a way that their readers are
uplifted by it." Wilder allows us to watch this formulation as it is embodied in Catullus's outcries, in his letters
to his beloved, his poems, and the talk about him.
Through "colliding" with Clodia—no "ordinary" woman
—Catullus creates extraordinary art.

The Ides of March takes its place alongside *The
Bridge of San Luis Rey* as a novel of destiny, human lim-
itation, and the worth of intense feeling. Informed by
more complex ideas and written in a more abrupt style,
it necessarily engages fewer readers. Its reputation will
probably rise as it comes to be seen as a clearer expression of the problem Wilder posed in the 1920s. The
problem of Providence in *the Bridge*, handled so ironically and slyly, is here faced head on. Quite blunt in its
existentialist conclusion about "why"—"we are all at the
mercy of a falling tile"—it also preaches an honest admiration of the unknown. But as he draws back from athe-
ism, total determinism, and nihilism, Wilder also loses
readers who view him an an uncritical, old-fashioned op-
timist. His Caesar, however, is filled with doubt and

faith, self-criticism and self-confidence, distrust and wonder. When readers recognize this complexity, they will receive the novel more sensitively.[7]

The Eighth Day—Wilder's last full-scale exploration of man's place in the cosmos—is a hulking book that contrasts sharply in its design and texture with *The Ides of March*. After almost twenty years, Wilder returned to the novel form and to a posture of wonder and awe. The intervening years had not been among his best, and this wide-ranging work has the quality of a great compensatory statement, a narrative so crammed with ideas and people that it seems devised to counterbalance the sparseness of the 1950s and early 1960s. The new book is also another foray into new territory—no repeat of the hothouse atmosphere of *The Cabala* and *The Bridge*, it returns to American folksiness and local color, but blends them with exotic scenes from Chile and St. Kitts as well as heavily applied ideas about destiny and purpose.

John Ashley, an engineer in Coaltown, Illinois, is tried for the murder of his business associate, Breckenridge Lansing, found guilty, and sentenced to death. Just as the innocent Ashley is being transported for the carrying out of the sentence, he is abducted. In terms of sheer plot line, the mystery becomes both a conventional search for the killer and an attempt to discover why Ashley was saved and by whom. This rather ordinary material—handled, it should be added, in a rambling manner totally inappropriate to the usual pleasures of mystery fiction—becomes a pretext for a much more profound investigation, an analytic treatment of Ashley's creative and resourceful nature, his family's endurance and eventual success, and the trying circumstances that surround the world's progressive men and women. A book that gives the initial impression of being a mystery soon wends its way into metaphysical meditation.[8]

The plot thread concerns Ashley's wandering in New Orleans and Chile, his ingenious methods of survival, and his eventual vindication; interspersed with this is the larger philosophical search—essentially Wilder's pursuit of people's origins and the sources of their destinies. In six loosely structured chapters he studies two families—those of the victim and of the accused murderer—and their place in the universal order.

In a letter to Robert Hutchins quoted by Gilbert Harrison, Wilder urged his friend to understand Goethe's view of our situation: "All nature strives to bring every detail to its truest expression of its function. All nature is working *for* you. Rise above immediate things and feel that—get a-holt of that. Float in the teleological tide."[9] The conviction that the world makes sense, that human activity is purposeful, is the informing idea of *The Eighth Day*. The narrative concerns people living up to their natures, conspiring with both good luck and adversity to reach goals, lifting themselves out of disillusionment and misfortunes. Once again, the novel seems to revive the problems of Wilder's first works: accident, providence, the wellsprings of human action. Like *The Ides of March*, it is more forceful and unambiguous about its conviction that people create the world's meaning and are not mere victims of neurosis or falling bridges. As John Ashley proves his moral and intellectual worth through his engineering inventions, his clever strategies for saving his skin, and his dedication to work and family, he separates himself—like Caesar —from Wilder's early version of the insightful 1920s people who faced doom with no more than a few hasty realizations about love. When measured against the first two novels, *The Eighth Day* is altogether different in the way it approaches the question of purpose. But while *The Cabala* and *The Bridge* were in step with the 1920s and the poetry of desolation, *The Eighth Day* was not a book that accommodated itself to the America of 1967.[10]

John Ashley's strivings are intensely Protestant, have
the heavy aroma of the work ethic, and sometimes remind one of Horatio Alger. At a time when mass move-
ments and distrust of individualism were at their high
point, Wilder's story seemed strangely old-fashioned.
This effect, it should be noted, was probably further aggravated by his desire to stitch together the pattern of
his whole career in a long book: the novel is a kind of
summing up of past themes, a gathering together of all
his best motifs. Without offering anything new, it presents a lifetime of reflection in the new form of a large,
nineteenth-century-style novel of a family. Wilder had
always been the writer who excelled in short forms—exquisite portraitures, captured moments, episodes cleverly strung together. Here he has offered himself the
challenge of sustaining a book that contains all the stuff
of the realistic novel plus all his meditations. As it bursts
at the seams and strains to recreate the textures of so
many lives, the novel sometimes breaks down.

The weaknesses of *The Eighth Day* are very much
connected with its ambitiousness. There is almost nothing in his previous writing that Wilder does not try to
cram into this new narrative—and for this reason, the
book at first seems disordered and self-indulgent. Once
again, Wilder brings forward his ideas about accident,
chance, and causation. The epigrams and meditative
passages about John Ashley's fate come thick and fast.
"We were shaken into existence, like dice from a box."
John Ashley's abiding faith "is an ever-widening pool of
clarity, fed from springs beyond the margin of consciousness." These reflections take us back to *The Bridge*.
Then there are the replays of Wilder's cosmic ideas: in
Pullman Car Hiawatha the planets made their appearance in the play and counterpointed the ordinary routines of the train riders. In *The Eighth Day* there is a
scene in which Ashley tries to comfort young George
Breckenridge, a troubled boy whose rebelliousness, tal-

ent, and instability eventually drive him to patricide. As
Ashley looks out at the night sky, he tells George,
"We're going at that great speed and yet you saw how
quiet it is down there in the square. It's wonderful, isn't
it?" This "planetary consciousness," a term Wilder
coined in one of his lectures, pervades the book. In another episode, Ashley lies on the roof of his hotel in
Chile: "In infinite space, in infinite time, in infinite matter, an organism like a bubble is formed; it lasts a short
while and then bursts; and this bubble is myself." Wilder's field of reference has always been vast—but this
book goes on an uncontrolled exploration of man's place
in the cosmos. The rhetorical heights that he rises to
sometimes approach the inflations of Thomas Wolfe:
"Look about you in all directions—rise higher, rise
higher!—and see hills beyond hills, plains and rivers."
This reach toward the infinite, so typical of the overblown efforts of his first experimental one-act plays, accounts for part of the power of *The Eighth Day*, as well
as for a good deal of its floundering.

The musing about space and time and the pages of
talking become dangerously out of control when Wilder
starts to invent characters to absorb and carry the ideas.
The Ashleys and the Breckenridges are often convincing
enough—and generally hold our attention. But Wilder
generates too many unrealized people, types who are
walk-on philosophers meant to teach something and
then vanish. The most irritating among these are people
whom Roger Ashley meets in his steady rise to journalis-
tic fame in Chicago. Young Roger, thrown out on his
own after the family's humiliation, goes to seek his for-
tune and moves from hotel clerk to haberdashery salesman to hospital orderly to night clerk—and finally to
newspaperman. All along he is flanked by mentors and
advisors. There is Peter Bogardus, a fellow hospital
worker who promulgates ideas about reaching the
threshold of supreme happiness. There is Thomas Garri-

son Speidel, a crusty nihilist who tempts Roger with the prospect of an empty universe. And worst of all, there is a series of women and girls who impart fatuous worldly wisdom and clichés: one of them, a Japanese girl, tells Roger that he is freeing himself from everything that is bad in his karma. This girl says that when "I first knew you I thought that maybe you were a Bodhisattva." Fortunately Wilder recovers from this kind of heavily applied philosophizing and creates a few characters among Roger's friends who are genuinely realized and memorable. One of them, the Roman Catholic Archbishop of Chicago, is a finely drawn old man whose spirituality seems part of his nature and whose thoughts about the design in our life are both organic to the plot and interesting in themselves. In talking with Roger, he tells a story of some Chinese missionaries taken prisoner who pass messages from one cell to the other by tapping; some of those passing the code didn't know the meaning of the message. The little story is essentially a distillation of one of the novel's major themes: "We transmit (we hope) fairer things than we can fully grasp."

The remark might stand as the book's epigraph; it sums up John Ashley's bequeathing of faith and fortitude to his young family and it also describes Wilder's sense that there is a mysterious unity in our lives, a principle of coherence that makes the disparate endeavors of people conspire to achieve progress. Whereas the ill-assorted people of *The Cabala* and *The Bridge* conspire to generate love, the characters in *The Eighth Day* generate deeds. The title—denoting the day after the creation week, the time of a new beginning and new acts —is intended to describe the active lives of the Ashley family members. The book comes to be about the organic filaments that connect the deeds of one generation with those of another. Wilder—without a tincture of irony or a measure of distance—is involved with the way young Ashleys work out the family destiny by rising to

distinction in their careers. John Ashley, a humorless
doer who has an "inner quiet" that allows him to ignore
the distractions of his bad luck and limitations, has built
a world of meaning for himself through his hard work as
an engineer and through the works of his children. His
puttering with mechanical devices yields inventions that
eventually provide for needy children in the next generation. (Recall Mrs. Webb's legacy in *Our Town*, a less-
vigorous image of creativity and generosity.) Another
man of action like Caesar who has contempt for irresolu-
tion and idle musing, Ashley is, unfortunately, too much
the exemplar; rather uncomplex when compared with
the tormented Roman dictator, he seems stripped of the
doubts and fears that make Caesar a subtly fashioned
person.

The stories of Ashley's children deflect attention
from this weakness in portrayal, but they do not overcome it. Roger's integrity as a man and his creativity as a
journalist surveying urban life make him a precisely designed inheritor of his father's faith, but not altogether a
gripping character. There are times when he seems like
a stolid burgher—perhaps Wilder's embodiment of
characteristics that his father Amos would have admired.
Despite a flurry of sexual affairs and a tendency to
change his job, Roger becomes conventionally successful
and all too much his father's son. His flat personality
seems to be one of the Ashley family heirlooms—his father, John, journeys through trying times in the Americas without showing a glimpse of humor, cynicism, or
worldly resentment; his mother is the type of woman
whose capacity for lonely enduring and self-containment
seems like the best and dullest of German virtues. Roger
inherits both parents' practical vision: at times it seems
as if his fortitude is an old-fashioned conception of "character" raised several powers by Wilder's ardor.

The Ashley women provide one exception to Wilder's rather forced portrayal of virtues. Sophia, the

second-oldest daughter, is a true Ashley in her faith and dedication to practical work; yet somehow she seems alive as a person in a way that the others do not. In the first long chapter, called "'The Elms' 1885–1905," Sophia is featured as the family member who keeps the spirit of hope from dying in the humiliated Ashley household. While Mrs. Ashley has removed herself and the girls from all contact with the stony community, Sophia conceives a plan to start a boardinghouse. In a series of scenes that are quite poignant and arresting, we see the young girl struggling to turn the family fortunes around. "Nourished" by "those two distant outcasts, her father and her brother," the girl transforms simple acts—selling lemonade at a train station, bargaining to get old furniture, convincing her irritatingly righteous mother—into very memorable episodes. Like the soda-fountain scene in *Our Town,* or the other moments of ordinary life, Sophia's understated actions become emblems of old-fashioned decency and care. The line that separates this representation of people from the sentimentalist's view will, of course, have to be determined by the reader. Some may find that Sophia's self-sacrificing nature and her freedom from the resentments and frustrations of adolescence are all too ideal. But others may recognize the matter-of-fact quality in Wilder's descriptions of Sophia's work. The other Ashley portraits are damaged by Wilder insistent rhetoric of faith and hope, but this portrait, which does indeed contain much forced material, is nevertheless moving and genuine because of Wilder's ability to return us to the resonant world of *Our Town* with its routines, daily chores, and pleasures. The other children in the Ashley household—Lily, who becomes a great singer, journalist Roger, and Constance, who has a career as a major social reformer—are so loaded down with extraordinary gifts that they sink as human beings. Sophia, by contrast, takes her place next to Emily in *Our Town* and Ma Kirby

in *The Happy Journey to Trenton and Camden:* Wilder
kindles another affecting portrait from the plain materials of a limited environment. The girl's awkward sales
pitch to a neighbor contains some of the spirit of Wilder's unassuming prose: "My mother opened a boardinghouse at 'The Elms'—you can see it behind those trees.
We have dinner at twelve o'clock. It's thirty-five cents,
but if you come every day of the week you'd get one dinner free. My mother's a wonderful cook."

As usual with Wilder, there are strange overtones
to the book that complicate the progressive drift of his
narrative. Those who would jump to the conclusion that
The Eighth Day is a sappy success story should consider
his 1960s admixtures of tragedy and grim realism. Wilder cleverly remarked that the story is like Louisa May
Alcott as "mulled over" by Dostoevski;[11] and indeed,
Wilder does lay on the domestic virtues and coziness
with equal measures of anguish and dread. Mrs. Ashley
presides over a troubled and desperately lonely household; a principled and hard-working woman, she is also a
loveless and distant parent who is wrapped up in her
love for John Ashley and her vision of her own importance. Sophia cracks emotionally from the strain of over-
work and the tensions of isolation. Lily and Roger love
their home but leave it without much hesitation. Meanwhile, Mother Beata goes on working and living—quite
indifferent to the concerns of those around her. In this
portrait Wilder has told a truth about the rigors and inju-
ries of a Protestant household—perhaps by way of describing some of the least attractive features of life with
his father. He has also shown the cost of Beata's rigidity
in Sophia's breakdown and eventual insanity—a connection that cannot help reflecting on the anguishing circumstances of Wilder's own sister Charlotte's mental
troubles and eventual collapse and death. For all its
hope and hard work, the Ashley household has also produced its measure of tragedy and derailed promise.

Even the "successful" children spend time reflecting on the lack of affection in their home.

The most disturbing insights into the desperation of the American home are to be found in Wilder's portraits of the Lansings. The central narrative thread of the novel—why Breckenridge Lansing has been murdered and by whom—gives Wilder the pretext to scrutinize the victim, his background, and his family. The evidence that drifts in points to a terrible, but usual, set of dramatic circumstances. Lansing is something of a failure, a macho extrovert whose job as manager of the Coaltown mines is a position that he fills incompetently. He tries to compensate for his inadequacy by being a hearty clubman, glad-hander, and petty tyrant. Unable to take hold in the larger world of work and achievement that John Ashley moves in with such ease and modesty, he takes to bullying his family. Wilder reaches for large generalizations about the social type that Lansing represents—the overbearing patriarch in a time of transition. The "majesty" of the patriarchal age began "cracking" at the end of the nineteenth century, and men like Breckenridge raged with frustration when they saw their power dissolving. As it deals with the conflicts of fathers and sons, wives and husbands, Wilder's portrayal of the Lansings is a fictional exploration of the troubling issues of his own youth: the overbearing father—here not a fine professional gentleman like Amos Wilder—taunts his sensitive son George; in this case the young boy is rebellious, strong-willed, and cracked—not at all the pliant and well-balanced Thornton. A lover of Russian culture and an outsider in Coaltown, George is pushed to his limit by his conventional father.

He snaps mentally—like Sophia. He shoots his father, believing, not without foundation, that Lansing is abusing his mother. Wilder overcomes the hokey melodramatic aspects of this material by making George Lansing one of his most anguished and complex charac-

ters. Although his father is a mean-spirited and often
hypocritical version of George Brush or George Antrobus, a noisy champion of the American domestic virtues,
George Lansing represents doubt, resentment, and vulnerability. The reign of the patriarch-tyrant has un-
hinged him and made him unfit for an American home.
He loses all faith in the role of the American male and
eventually runs away to Russia where he pursues an extraordinary career as an actor. A protean figure like
Theophilus North, he gains recognition for his ability to
play an amazing range of parts. George, who thinks of
himself as a man of the eighth day, begins a new life
disengaged from family and friends. After having gone
through a hellish period following the Coaltown murder
scene—George's mind and memory are so disordered
that he winds up in an asylum—he realizes his dream of
escape from America, the English language, and his
middle-class home by traveling to Russia and rising to
prominence on the stage; he transcends the world of his
father, even though such transcendence must involve
murder, agony, and repentance. George Lansing is a
more fully developed, highly charged, and clearly motivated version of Henry Antrobus in *The Skin of Our
Teeth*. Both youths are enraged by authority, driven to
violence, and motivated by personal injury. Though
Henry Antrobus was conceived in time of war and is an
essentially horrifying embodiment of the death instinct,
a fascist bred in the bosom of a New Jersey family,
George is essentially a tragic portrait of the creative personality, an embodiment of the distructive instincts that
must exert themselves so that the artist may free himself
from the bonds of patriarchs. George Lansing must kill
his father in order to become a self. Although Wilder
was deeply resentful of the suggestion that there is a par-
ricidal strain in his writings[12] (perhaps because his feelings for Amos Wilder were ambivalent rather than consciously hostile), he was not able to erase the motifs of

his plays and novels: Henry lashing out at his father, the comic scenes involving children wishing for their parents' deaths, Vandergelder's overbearing paternalism, or the Romans' hatred of Caesar. Wilder's characters are caught up in resentments that range in form from dreams to violent actions.

The atmosphere of *The Eighth Day*—settings in working-class Chile, New Orleans, middle-class Hoboken, combined with constant references to the cosmic order—should be no surprise to his readers. Once again—as in *Heaven's My Destination* and *Theophilus North*—Wilder seems too restless to concentrate on one place. His energies radiate out to exotic St. Kitts and the story of Eustachia Lansing (née Sims), to Ashley's life among the workers in a mining town in Chile, to the bourgeois routines of Coaltown and Hoboken, to the Chicago of the ambitious Roger. But because of his spacious and detailed treatment of destinies, Wilder becomes something he has never been before—a realistic chronicler who dwells on the formative influences in people's lives. All his previous novels—and *Theophilus North*, which appeared in 1973—have a rapid pace, an episodic structure, and a evocative rendering of places. *The Eighth Day* stands out in its nineteenth-century proportions and its meticulous attempts to record. The fantasies, evocations, and picaresque romps of the past are abandoned for a steady viewing of just about everything concerning the Ashleys and the Lansings. The result is a very obvious slackening in concentration and power. A novelist who trained himself in the discipline of the short work—especially the work that frees itself from the constraints of realism and verisimilitude—is likely to have trouble with the mode of Tolstoy and Trollope. Wilder only succeeds in bringing Coaltown to life because of the interest of Sophia's story and because of the small resonant details of town life that recall *Our Town*. Added to these details is the cosmic–geological evaluation of the place—a look at the terrain that reminds us of the professor's lecture about Grover's Corners. Again, numbers proliferate, as do references to dinosaurs and primitive inhabitants. This time the effect is not quite right—a replay that seems strained, almost prefabricated. Although the geological backdrop is appropriate for the novel's overall theme of progression, it leads Wilder into the trap of overdoing and overreaching: the cosmic insistence of the prose loses the natural quality that such musings had in *Our Town* or even in *Pullman Car Hiawatha*. Detached from scenes and characters, such philosophizing palls.

Another possible influence that Wilder was grappling with was suggested in a characteristically frank letter from Edmund Wilson to his friend Helen Muchnic. "It stirred me more than anything I have read since *Zhivago*—though it is not really so remarkable—and I wonder whether it may not have been partly inspired by Pasternak."[13] Wilson was doubtless pointing to a theme and to the novel's design: like *Zhivago*, *The Eighth Day* is a romantic celebration of its characters' capacities for living and intense feeling; it is charged by the same ardor and love for landscapes, appetite for experience, and unresentful acceptance of pain and loss. Wilder's canvas is enormous; he traces generations, establishes continuity, and studies legacies of temperament and mind that are similar to Pasternak's cosmic explorations. And yet—the book is "not really so remarkable." Pasternak's historical penetration, lyrical genius, and Tolstoyan characterization may well have inspired Wilder, but they cannot help making us see his defects.

In trying to infuse *The Eighth Day* with more ideas and emotions than its characters could credibly embody, Wilder made one of several major mistakes of his career. Attempting to be Tolstoy, Dostoevski, Alcott, Pasternak, and himself all at once, he succeeded only in short stretches; and yet the uneven quality of the book should not obscure its place in the Wilder canon—it is a rounding off of themes that he had been working with for years, a dense and leisurely investigation of what his mind was burdened with. While *The Ides of March* succeeds on all levels because of its craftsmanship and its mastery of material, *The Eighth Day* reaches for too much. But the failure is part of Wilder's literary nature —what his brother Amos once called his "total humanistic outreach."[14]

Epilogue

"AT-HOMENESS IN EXISTENCE"

"'Culture' is in me a second nature," Wilder once said. He takes his place as a writer who is unashamed of his passionate enthusiasms and his incorporations. At home with what his contemporaries were thinking, unresentful of other styles and sensibilities, Wilder never insulated his imagination from either the nourishments or the corruptions of his age. Accessible to the currents of modern philosophy and social thought, he was the least resistant of artists.

While isolation was one of the major themes of his work, friendly exchange was his characteristic way of conducting a career. Wilder immersed himself in the work and thought of congenial as well as alien figures and delved deeply into their writing to find what was universal. Dismissing the early critical notion that Samuel Beckett was a negative writer, Wilder, the seventy-eight-year-old working writer, was as open to new avenues of expression as he had been when he apprenticed himself in the early twenties to Proust and Joyce:

I reread some Beckett lately—the "Molloy" and the "Mercier and [Camier]?" with an increased admiration. Now that I am moving into the age-bracket that has always been an obsessive image with him (I'm 78) I recognize how piercingly sharp his evocation is. . . . I don't creep on my hands and feed [illegible], but these things are incidental. As for his total negation of what life offers—I just regard that as *his* "fiction." To write, I feel, capture as magnificently as that is to make a smashing affirmation. My word for S. Beckett is purity—purity of the polished lens.[1]

The American critic Guy Davenport has described the creative process in such a way as to clarify Wilder's literary nature: in an essay called "The Geography of the Imagination," Davenport analyzes how artists borrow ideas and motifs from other artists and from alien cultures; the metamorphic quality of the imagination then reshapes this material, making it the writer's or painter's property. And yet the individual creator, Edgar Allan Poe, for instance, is never far from his sources, whether they are easily identifiable books and ideas or deep-rooted influences that he is unconscious of. Davenport speaks of Poe,—one of American literature's great adapters—much as we have described Wilder: "Poe's imagination was perfectly at home in geographies he had no knowledge of except what his imagination appropriated from other writers. We might assume, in ignorance, that he knew Paris like a Parisian, that Italy and Spain were familiar to him, and even Antarctica and the face of the moon."[2] Such a feeling of at-homeness with the distant, the exotic, and the apparently unclaimable is the characteristic that accounts for Wilder's powerfully different quality as a writer of the Americas.

In *The Journals* Wilder himself wrote about Poe's borrowings and the nature of his imagination: the description that he gives of the classic American writer reaches Davenport's conclusion—and might well serve to describe much of Wilder's own work. "Poe's imagination, no more than that of most of us, could not furnish him images other than those he had already seen in picture books, theater, etc." Or put more colorfully, "His head was filled, like the bedchamber of Ligeia's widower, with Gothic-Druidic-Saracenic lumber."[3] If we expand these influences to capture Wilder's wide field of enthusiasms, the conclusion remains the same. Jorge Luis Borges is another imaginative voyager who is at once very much an Argentine, as Wilder is a bourgeois American, and at the same time an artist who is at home in conjured settings and hothouse atmospheres that abandon the territory reported on by realistic storytellers.

Such an approach had its dangers for Wilder's development. Just as Papa moved him from new situation to new situation, modern culture and the literature of the ages often unsettled him and made him take the wrong path. His "Kafka" play, *The Emporium*, was a foray into an alienated world that was ultimately impossible for a writer who believed in progress, redemptive emotions, and coherence. He even confessed that he was mistakenly "drawn into the Kafka hero, the frustrated pre-condemned struggler. That is not my bent; I'm not the stuff of which nihilists are made."[4] Although he could work well with the motifs of Joyce and Proust —two essentially orderly and affirmative artists—he panicked when it came to entering the defeated and self-doubting world of Kafka. While not the sententious yea saying playwright and novelist that he is often dismissed as, he was at some distance from the radical negativity of a writer who believed one could never reach the castle. The part of Kafka's world that was "real" to him—"the seduction and the ambiguity and the terror of the Absolute"—sounds more like his own uses of existentialism in *The Ides of March* or his wonder and irony in *The Bridge of San Luis Rey*.

Strangely enough, his relationship with the Greek classical tradition also led to a misfire. *The Woman of Andros* is saved from disaster by Wilder's deft touch and by his clever and moving use of Platonism; but when he returned to the classical world in *The Alcestiad*, something went wrong with his transformative powers: the play—which was a stage debacle—has all the familiar

themes—love, self-sacrifice, the yearning for coherence. But the characters lie heavily on the pages, posture, and declaim, and are altogether unfit to be placed
beside the live people in *Our Town,* the short plays, or
The Skin of Our Teeth. Special pleading is needed to
find a way to overlook the lapses. Although his Roman
portraits in *The Ides of March* use the counterpointing of
trivial gossip and terror, the people in *The Alcestiad* are
moved forward only by ponderous language and vague
dissolving motivations. Fortunately, Wilder did not
choose to pursue the classical-mythological vein; and fortunately Mike Gold was no longer watching him. The
"catalytic"[5] element that one observer saw in Wilder's
use of Joyce and Proust was obviously absent from the
story of Alcestis; despite the fact that she leaves a legacy
of love, she remains as an awkward figure among his
characters.

One kind of drama that he continued to remain at
home with was the story of disaster and turmoil set ironically in an *Our Town*-like atmosphere. Alfred Hitchcock
hired him to work on the screenplay of *Shadow of a
Doubt,* a film about a pathological killer who returns to
his hometown of Santa Rosa, California, and attempts to
pass as solicitous and generous Uncle Charlie to his innocent niece. The Wilder imprint is on the film in its details, its folksiness, and its creeping dread. Uncle Charlie is the "Merry Widow" killer, we later learn—a man
who has done away with numbers of rich women because he perceived them as useless, parasitic, fat, and
ugly. The grizzly situation of a tormented madman is
rendered in the colors of Wilder's America—dinner
with the family punctuated by Uncle Charlie's terrifying
remarks about the worthlessness of human life; busybody neighbors whose small concerns increase the tensions; a town of white-shingled houses and porches
where a man is harboring his destructive anguish.
Watching Uncle Charlie have dinner is likely to remind

the Wilder reader of other family scenes, especially
those in *The Long Christmas Dinner*. The early one-act
play was also concerned with the underside of human
lives, the hatred and torment that coexist casually with
domestic routine. Uncle Charlie is discovered by his
niece; he attempts to kill the girl and falls from a moving
train. As all Santa Rosa comes to his funeral, the girl is
now the one to harbor the secret. This motif of what we
do not know about those around us is threaded through
Wilder's career—in the loves of *The Bridge* and *The
Cabala,* in Mrs. Webb's legacy in *Our Town,* in *Our
Town's* central ideas about not seeing or realizing life's
value, in the distance between adults and children in
Childhood. *Shadow of a Doubt* is a small but significant
addition to this collection of painful secrets and missed
recognitions.

In 1956 Wilder worked on another drama about an
outsider's violently erupting consciousness. *The Wreck
of the 5:25* presents a man who, somewhat like Uncle
Charlie, comes back as a commuter to his suburban
home—but first peers into the window before entering
the living room. After a while, he appears as the husband and father—only to wind up an outsider again at
the end. He is seized by the police and found to be carrying a gun, presumably with which to kill himself. During the course of the action we find that he is a distillation of Wilder's unease about life in society: he fantasizes
about a train wreck and then about the total destruction
wrought by a nuclear holocaust (the latest version of a
falling bridge or the Ice Age), and yet he also resolves,
like the Marquesa and Mr. Antrobus, to affirm life and to
live more productively. The plot line here is sketchy and
a bit hysterical, suggesting that Wilder lost his grip on
craftsmanship in his urgent desire to convey a new version of his obsession with the lonely, self-destructive,
and dangerous individual. The play was shelved, but the
impulse lived on, finding its way into the character of

George Lansing in *The Eighth Day*. It is yet another example of the way in which Wilder was on close terms with the darker side of the human condition.

The critics' neglect of Wilder—caused in part by his gentility, his lack of ideology, his failed experiments, his protean nature—is probably also a result of the very nature of his humanistic outreach. At home in existence —as John Ashley was in *The Eighth Day*—he was not permanently at home with a literary form or special atmosphere or mode for a long enough time to become its unquestioned master. Wilder never quite lost the youthful impulsiveness and literary hubris that caused him to plan huge play cycles and make a few startling attempts. His later works never lack ardor and life, but they very often have the mark of the apprentice learning how to present his characters. They are many American writers of the postwar period who could explore the characters and situations of Wilder's Coaltown with more subtlety and less insistent rhetoric. But it is difficult to think of more than a few who have Wilder's intellectual range. It also is not a challenge to name American writers who wear their alienation like badges of honor; yet we are hard pressed to think of a writer who combines irony and gentle acceptance of existence in Wilder's way. Despite the frustrations of youth, the slings of his detractors, the false starts and abandoned projects, he retained a guarded confidence about himself and his world. For almost fifty years he continued to show what he felt about isolation and torment, joy and wonder.

Notes

1. THE SKIN OF HIS TEETH

1. Quoted in Gilbert Harrison's *The Enthusiast: A Life of Thornton Wilder* (New Haven and New York: Ticknor and Fields, 1983), p.302. On Wilder's European qualities see also Richard Goldstone, *Thornton Wilder: An Intimate Portrait* (New York: Saturday Review Press, 1975), p.257.
2. Goldstone, p.18.
3. Harrison, p.6.
4. Ibid.
5. Ibid., p.23.
6. Ibid., p.29.
7. Ibid., p.23.
8. Goldstone, p.23.
9. Ibid., p.19.
10. Harrison, p.50.
11. Ibid., pp.53–54.
12. Ibid., p.68.
13. Ibid., p.76.
14. Ibid., p.92.
15. Edmund Wilson, "Thornton Wilder," *The Shores of Light* (New York: Farrar, Straus and Giroux, 1952), p.388.
16. Ibid., p.391.
17. *Writers at Work: The Paris Review Interviews*, ed. Malcolm Cowley (New York: Viking, 1958), p.104.
18. Harrison, p.108.
19. Wilson, "A Weekend at Ellerslie," *The Shores of Light*, p.379.
20. Harrison, p.167.
21. Michael Gold, "Wilder: Prophet of the Genteel Christ," *New Republic*, October 22, 1930, pp.226–267.

22. Philip Rahv, *Literature and the Sixth Sense* (Boston: Houghton Mifflin, 1969), pp.1–7.
23. Linda Simon, *Thornton Wilder: His World* (Garden City, New York: Doubleday, 1979), pp.95–96.
24. *Writers at Work,* p.104.
25. Wilson, "Mr. Wilder in the Midwest," *The Shores of Light,* p.588.
26. Quoted by Harrison, p.138.
27. Ibid., p.137.
28. Ibid., p.160.
29. On Wilder's visit to Vienna, see Harrison, pp.139–140. Also Simon, pp.118–119.
30. Harrison, p.140.
31. Ibid., p.160.
32. Ibid., p.183.
33. On the erosion of the play's integrity see Simon, p.234.
34. *The Journals of Thornton Wilder 1939–1961,* ed. Donald Gallup (New Haven: Yale University Press, 1985). Wilder became a fairly steady journal keeper in this period; his earlier journal entries are not yet available.
35. Harrison, Chapter 19.
36. Joseph Campbell and Henry Morton Robinson, "The Skin of Whose Teeth?" *Saturday Review of Literature,* December 19, 1942, pp.3–4, and February 13, 1943, pp.16, 18–19.
37. Edmund Wilson, "The Antrobuses and the Earwickers," *Classics and Commercials* (New York: Farrar, Straus and Giroux, 1967), p.83.
38. Harrison, p.33.
39. Ibid., p.232.
40. Mary McCarthy, *"The Skin of Our Teeth," Sights and Spectacles: Theatre Chronicles 1937–1956* (New York: Meridian Books, 1957), pp.53–56.
41. Journals, pp.295–337.
42. Harrison, p.297.
43. Ibid., pp.279–280.
44. Ibid., p.330.
45. Amos Niven Wilder, *Thornton Wilder and His Public* (Philadelphia: Fortress Press, 1980), p.34.

46. Stanley Kauffmann, "Thornton Wilder," *The New Republic,* April 16, 1967, p.46.
47. Malcolm Cowley, "A Unique Case," *The Flower and the Leaf: A Contemporary Record of American Writing Since 1941* (New York: Viking, 1945), p.312.
48. Granville Hicks, review of *Theophilus North, New York Times Book Review,* October 21, 1973, p.16.
49. Malcolm Cowley quoted by Amos Wilder, p.72. Remarks appeared in *New York Times Book Review,* December 21, 1975, p.20.
50. Benjamin DeMott, "Old Fashioned Innovator," *New York Times Book Review,* April 2, 1967, pp.1, 51.
51. Francis Fergusson, "Three Allegorists: Brecht, Wilder and Eliot," *The Human Image in Dramatic Literature* (Garden City: Doubleday, 1957), p.60.

2. Isolation in Wilder's Foreign Novels

1. Gilbert Harrison notes that Wilder had been reading Proust since his Berkeley High School days. See p.31.
2. See Goldstone, p.47.
3. See Wilson, "Thornton Wilder," p.390, for a mythic interpretation.
4. On Samuele's lack of qualities see Malcolm Goldstein, *The Art of Thornton Wilder* (Lincoln, Nebraska: University of Nebraska Press, 1965), p.39.
5. See below for the connection between this idea and Proust's world.
6. Wilson, "Thornton Wilder," p.385.
7. For other negative criticism besides Gold see especially Goldstein's remarks, p.68; and Simon's quotation from Henry Hazlitt, p.75. Hazlitt found Wilder's new book "an exercise in style."
8. See also Goldstein, who objects to the "torpid" romantic prose, p.68.
9. Wilson, "Dahlberg, Dos Passos, and Wilder," *The Shores of Light,* p.445.
10. Rex Burbank makes a similar point in *Thornton Wilder* (New York: Twayne, 1961), p.60.

3. Strange Discipline

1. Harrison, p.38.
2. On Wilder's use of existentialism see Chapter 6.
3. Donald Haberman, *The Plays of Thornton Wilder: A Critical Study* (Middletown, Connecticut: Wesleyan University Press, 1967), p.104.
4. A. R. Gurney's *The Dining Room* (New York: Dramatists Play Service, Inc., 1982) is a fine contemporary work that has marked similarities to Wilder's play: time and change give both dramas their substance; both also use the dining room as the locus for the American family's problems.
5. On the themes of the play see Goldstein, p.81.
6. On these fragments see *Journals,* pp.280–283.
7. Wilder's connection with the Theater of the Absurd involves his affinities with several writers. He was always impressed with Beckett's economical elegance (see Epilogue). Beckett's dramatization of incoherence and isolation might well have been one force that brought Wilder back into the theater in the late 1950s with plays about the terrors and absurdities of infancy and childhood. Wilder also got Alan Schneider to direct *Godot* and therefore had a part in Beckett's international success. Wilder's own plays seem to have had a particular influence on the early careers of both Edward Albee and Israel Horovitz; with Albee one can see the stylized, highly critical version of America, complete with the grotesque family members in *The Skin* and *The American Dream.* With Horovitz—a personal friend of the elderly Wilder—one can see the playful, experimental side of Wilder, the use of jokes and stage conceits.

4. The Major Full-Length Plays

1. Goldstone, p.140.
2. Mary McCarthy, "Class Angles and a Wilder Classic," *Sights and Spectacles* (New York: Farrar, Straus and Cudahy, 1956), pp.27–29.
3. Quoted by Linda Simon, p.144.

4. Ibid., p.143. Wilder's 1938 letter is in the Beinecke Collection; Wilson's 1940 letter is in *Letters on Literature and Politics 1912–1972*, edited by Elena Wilson, foreword by Leon Edel, introduction by Daniel Aaron (New York: Farrar, Straus and Giroux, 1977), p.185.

5. Wilder, "Prefaces to *Three Plays: Our Town, The Skin of Our Teeth, The Matchmaker*," in *American Characteristics and Other Essays*, p.109.

6. See Jane Kallir, *The Folk Art Tradition* (New York: The Viking Press, 1981). This fine treatment presents the international view of the folk-art phenomenon. For a more analytic treatment of the folk style see Jean Lipman and Alice Winchester, *The Flowering of American Folk Art (1776–1876)* (New York: The Viking Press, 1974). Lipman and Winchester study the motifs of the folk artist, show how folk painters were not involved with the quaint and the nostalgic, and analyze the use of sharpened colors and simplified forms. They also deal with the fact that folk painters did not paint from nature—just as Wilder did not strive for realistic representation.

7. Louis Cazamian, *The Social Novel in England, 1830–1850: Dickens, Mrs. Gaskell, Disraeli, Kingsley* (London: Routledge and Kegan Paul, 1973).

8. Karl Marx, *The Economic and Philosophic Manuscripts of 1844*, 7th ed., Dirk Struik, trans. Martin Milligan (New York: International Publisher, 1964), pp.165–170.

9. Mary McCarthy, "The Skin of Our Teeth," *Sights and Spectacles*, pp.53–56.

10. *Journals*, p.22.

11. See also Douglas Wixon, Jr., "The Dramatic Techniques of Thornton Wilder and Bertolt Brecht," *Modern Drama*, XV, no. 2 (September 1972), pp.112–124. This informative essay gives special attention to the anti-illusionist theater of Brecht and Wilder; it argues that Wilder employed Brechtian techniques from 1931 onward. The article does not explore the thematic affinities of the two writers.

12. *Seven Plays* (Brecht), ed. Eric Bentley (New York: Grove Press, 1961).

13. Letter to Edmund Wilson (January 13, 1940), Beinecke Library.

14. Letter to Edmund Wilson (June 15, 1940), Beinecke Library.
15. Ibid.
16. Letter to Edmund Wilson (June 26, 1940), Beinecke Library.

5. FROM HEAVEN TO NEWPORT

1. On Protestantism in *Heaven's My Destination,* see Simon, p. 110.
2. Harrison, p. 149.
3. *Time* called Wilder a Prospero; *Newsweek* referred to Theophilus' power as "the sorcerer's wand."
4. See Granville Hicks, review of *Theophilus North, New York Times Book Review,* October 21, 1973, p. 1.

6. FLOATING IN THE TELEOLOGICAL TIDE

1. The complexity of Wilder's design was not appreciated by J. M. Lalley in *The New Yorker,* February 21, 1948. Wilder's "liberties" and "lack of historical coherence" ruined the overall effect of the book.
2. On Caesar as an existentialist hero see Harrison, p. 252.
3. See the preface to *The Ides of March* (New York: Harper and Brothers, 1948), vii.
4. Cowley, p. 311.
5. For Wilder's attitudes toward the existentialists see Journal entries on Kierkegaard, Sartre, Camus, Maritain. Wilder worked on a play in 1953 called "The Heir," a drama about "the Existentialist man who, in words Camus quoted to me from Dostoyevski, is afraid that he doesn't hate everything enough." This strain in existentialist thought was not, evidently, congenial—the project was jettisoned.
6. On Sheldon's nature see Harrison, p. 161.
7. Two unsympathetic responses to *The Ides* can be found in *The New Republic,* March 1, 1948, p. 22; and *The Christian Science Monitor,* February 18, 1948, p. 14. A review in *Time* (February 23, 1948) was also insensitive to Wil-

der's methods, but at least admitted that he was a master of "the unexpected."

8. It was this quality in the book that caused Stanley Kauffmann to denounce it in *The New Republic*.

9. Harrison, p.370. D. J. Gordon in *The Yale Review* (October 1967, p.107) felt this "teleological urgency" was what marred the characters in *The Eighth Day*.

10. Malcolm Cowley commented generally on Wilder's odd insensitivity to America's moods—"His work is untimely in a spectacular fashion." Not entirely applicable to the Wilder of *The Bridge* or even *Our Town*, the remark does seem appropriate to the late works. Richard Goldstone makes a similar point about the success of *The Bridge* and the neglect of *The Eighth Day*, p.248.

11. Harrison, p.344.

12. Amos Wilder (pp.15–16) frowns on Richard Goldstone's conclusions about Thornton's resentment of his father; while no one would ever accuse Goldstone of examining the issue with subtlety, the tensions of the father-son relationship are evident in much of Wilder's work and tend to support Goldstone's suggestions.

13. Edmund Wilson, *Letters on Literature and Politics 1912–1972*, selected and edited by Elena Wilson (New York: Farrar, Straus and Giroux, 1977), p.670.

14. Amos Wilder, p.35.

Epilogue

1. Quoted from a letter to Luann Walther, a New York editor and friend (July 6, 1975).

2. Guy Davenport, *The Geography of the Imagination* (San Francisco: North Point Press, 1981), p.9.

3. *Journals*, p.197.

4. Ibid., p.334.

5. Carl Balliett, "The Skin of Whose Teeth?: Part III," *The Saturday Review*, January 2, 1943, p.11.

Selected Bibliography

MAJOR WORKS BY THORNTON WILDER

The Cabala. New York: A. & C. Boni, 1926.

The Bridge of San Luis Rey. New York: A. & C. Boni, 1927.

The Angel That Troubled the Waters and Other Plays. New York: Coward-McCann, 1928.

The Woman of Andros. New York: A. & C. Boni, 1930.

The Long Christmas Dinner and Other Plays in One Act. New Haven: Yale University Press, 1931.

Heaven's My Destination. New York: Harper & Row, 1935.

The Merchant of Yonkers. New York: Harper & Brothers, 1939.

The Ides of March. New York: Harper & Brothers, 1948.

Three Plays: Our Town, The Skin of Our Teeth, The Matchmaker. New York: Harper & Brothers, 1957.

The Eighth Day. New York: Harper & Row, 1967.

Theophilus North. New York: Harper & Row, 1973.

The Alcestiad, or a Life in the Sun. New York: Harper & Row, 1977.

American Characteristics and Other Essays. Edited by Donald Gallup, foreword by Isabel Wilder. New York: Harper & Row, 1979.

The Journals of Thornton Wilder 1939–1961. Selected and edited by Donald Gallup. New Haven: Yale University Press, 1985.

UNPUBLISHED WRITINGS

Thornton Wilder's unpublished work—play drafts, letters, journals—is housed in the Collection of American Literature at the Beinecke Rare Book and Manuscript Library, Yale University.

SECONDARY SOURCES

Atkinson, Brooks. "Mr. Wilder's Roman Fantasia." *New York Times Book Review*, February 22, 1948, pp.1,30.

Balliet, Carl, Jr. "The Skin of Whose Teeth?" Part III. *Saturday Review of Literature* 26 (January 2, 1943):11.

Brown, E. K. "A Christian Humanist." *University of Toronto Quarterly* 4 (April 1935):356–370.

Burbank, Rex. *Thornton Wilder*. New York: Twayne, 1961.

Campbell, Joseph, and Robinson, H. M. "The Skin of Whose Teeth?" *Saturday Review of Literature* 25 (December 19, 1942):3–4, 26 (February 15, 1943):16–18.

Cowley, Malcolm. *The Flower and the Leaf*. Ed. Donald Faulkner. New York: Viking, 1985.

Davenport, Guy. *The Geography of the Imagination*. San Francisco: North Point Press, 1981.

Fergusson, Francis. "Three Allegorists: Brecht, Wilder and Eliot." *The Human Image in Dramatic Literature*. Garden City: Doubleday, 1957, pp.41–72.

Fuller, Edmund. "Thornton Wilder: The Notation of the Heart." *American Scholar* 28 (Spring 1959):210–217.

Fulton, A. R. "Expressionism Twenty Years After." *Sewanee Review* 52 (Summer 1944):398–413.

Gold, Michael. "Wilder: Prophet of a Genteel Christ." *New Republic*, October 22, 1930, pp.266–267.

Goldstein, Malcolm. *The Art of Thornton Wilder*. Omaha: University of Nebraska Press, 1965.

Goldstone, Richard H. *Thornton Wilder: An Intimate Portrait*. New York: Saturday Review Press, 1975.

Grebanier, Bernard. *Thornton Wilder*. Minneapolis: University of Minnesota Press, 1964.

Haberman, Donald. *The Plays of Thornton Wilder*. Middletown, Connecticut: Wesleyan University Press, 1967.

Harrison, Gilbert A. *The Enthusiast: A Life of Thornton Wilder*. New Haven and New York: Ticknor and Fields, 1983.

Hicks, Granville. Review of *Theophilus North*. *New York Times Book Review*, October 21, 1973, pp.1,16.

Kauffmann, Stanley. "Thornton Wilder," *The New Republic*, April 6, 1967, p.26.

Kuner, M. C. *Thornton Wilder: The Bright and the Dark*. New York: Crowell, 1972.

Lalley, J. M. "Help, Ho! They Murder Caesar!" *The New Yorker*, February 21, 1948, p.91.

McCarthy, Mary. *Sights and Spectacles: Theatre Chronicles 1937–1956*. New York: Meridian Books, 1957.

"Obliging Man, An." *Time*, January 12, 1953, pp.44–49.

Rahv, Philip. *Literature and the Sixth Sense*. Boston: Houghton Mifflin, 1969.

Scott, Winfield Townley. *"Our Town* and the Golden Veil." *Virginia Quarterly* 29 (January 1953):103–117.

Simon, Linda. *Thornton Wilder: His World*. Garden City, New York: Doubleday, 1979.

Watts, Richard. Review of *The Ides of March*. *The New Republic*, March 1, 1948, p.22.

Wilder, Amos Niven. *Thornton Wilder and His Public*. Philadelphia: Fortress Press, 1980.

Wilson, Edmund. *Classics and Commercials*. New York: Farrar, Straus and Giroux, 1950.

Wilson, Edmund. *Letters on Literature and Politics 1912–1972*. New York: Farrar, Straus and Giroux, 1977.

Wilson, Edmund. *The Shores of Light*. New York: Farrar, Straus and Giroux, 1952.

Wixson, Douglas Charles, Jr. "The Dramatic Techniques of Thornton Wilder and Bertolt Brecht: A Study in Comparison," *Modern Drama* XV (September 1972) no.2.

Index